The *Lazy* Vegetable Grower

by John Yeoman

Village Guild

Published by:

The Village Guild Ltd,

The Old School House,

Ivinghoe Aston, Leighton Buzzard,

Beds LU7 9DP, UK

Fax/phone: 01525 221492

E-mail: john@villageguild.co.uk

Printed on chlorine-free, environmentally friendly paper from sustainable resources, using toxin-free inks. This book may be safely composted, if torn into fragments, mixed with lawn clippings or manure then danced upon with football boots.

ISBN: 0-9542006-1-6

Preface

This little book is a faithful and true record of my experiments in growing edible plants of every kind outdoors organically, in a totally *inhospitable* environment in the UK, zone 8.

> I mean... bad soil, hardpan, Force 8 gales, the worst perennial weeds known in temperate climes, *plus snails....*

I evolved artful remedies galore, and all worked and grew me bountiful harvests, after a fashion.

Then I had a **Breakthrough** - a simple, totally free way to grow *any* vegetable whatsoever, in the worst soil imaginable (or even in no soil).

> Over five years, I tested it. And lo, *it worked!*

So I wrote this book

If you find my quirky ideas here too challenging, please relax. My advice will work, in *any* garden, even if... *you never, ever build a YeoPod.*

I have designed this book so the advice can help *any* organic gardener, anywhere, to improve the yield and quality they get from edible plants in their gardens.

> If you should also choose to use YeoPods, that's a magnificent (but optional) *bonus.* For you and your grandchildren to enjoy, in perpetuity..

Meanwhile, please enjoy my book.

And please take to your heart its - often strange - ideas. Though I may phrase them at times in humorous terms, I am always (at heart) passionately serious.

> Because... *the ideas work!*

I have the proof, growing outdoors now as I write. *In my own garden!*

Dedication

This book is dedicated to my wife Janice who has - for more than 20 years to date - endured with saintly patience the endless recycling of her kitchen utensils, nylon mesh curtains, wastebins, carpets, colanders, sieves, trousers, blouses, washing up bowls, socks and pantihose into unlikely garden applications.

Disclaimer

Mr Yeoman/The Village Guild Ltd disclaims all responsibility whatsoever for the use of any information or advice given or implied - or not given or implied - here or anywhere else, by himself/itself or by any other entity whatsoever.

Mrs Yeoman also disclaims all responsibility for Mr Yeoman and/or The Village Guild Ltd. Or for any other entity whatsoever.

For example... if any information here should ever be implicated in bringing your least favourite relative down with *fusarium wilt*, nobody will be held liable.

But Mr Yeoman *will* gratefully accept a bottle of vintage champagne...

Contents

Chapter 1
The birth of the YeoPod

Retirement to a country cottage!

What alluring visions it presented to my wife and I, those several years ago. Janice could play classical music all day and I could grow carrots, to insert in my ears.

The entire family might ramble at will through flowery meadows remote from technology and urban strife (always equipped with mobile phones, of course, lest we got lost).

And old John would have a big garden again after decades of living in cities where the only green thing was a traffic light.

Same as a pig's

After a gestation period of just four months, same as a pig's, our lawyer delivered us a Paddock. It came with two 18th century cottages knocked into one, umbilically attached to the paddock by a gravel path upon which - ancient covenants attest - we Must Not Build.

Our new estate measured ½ acre after rain but, such is the contractile nature of clay, only ¼ acre in dry weather.

We were now possessed of 0.62 of a hectare, or 100 rods, or 25 chains, and a growing area at its longest side - where our neighbour's brook babbled - of 15 perches or 200 cubits.

Alas, seed packets do not give planting distances in cubits but, I thought, I would doubtless muddle through.

So I was well pleased.

We all repaired to a restaurant to wet the baby's head (not least, because we hadn't yet worked out how to use the

Aga oven in the cottage). After a heated discussion in which I prevailed, we named it Yeoman's Croft.

We mailed Birth Announcements to everyone, including *The Times* and *Organic Gardening* magazine. Shortly afterwards an anonymous friend sent us a builder's sign **Yeoman's Croft** which he had found lying in a road. He said.

Gleefully, I hung it over the garden gate until Janice made me take it down.

A mirage

In the depths of Winter, Yeoman's Croft appeared a mirage of joys to come. Surrounded by ancient damson and elder trees, it had been so cropped by horses that it was as flat and green as a billiard table.

Behind it reared the historic tumulus of Ivinghoe Beacon, pockmarked with Stone Age forts.

Did my ancestors raise primitive crops there, millennia ago, I wondered? In kitchen gardens walled against wild boar and wolves?

Did they likewise smear rotten eggs on their fruit trees to deter deer?

Were they as afflicted as we are - with aphids and planning officers?

If so, I sympathised with them. They had no soap, in those days, to spray on aphids.

Surrounded by hope and history...

I began to plan the garden.

I bought a computer program, whereby I could plot every square inch with micrometric precision. Intercrops, catch crops, succession planting, rotations... *I missed nothing.*

Here in **Bed A** might be stubby carrots and broad beans, planted under cloches in March, followed by sweet corn and bush beans in June. Then swiss chard and Good King Henry could be sown in September (intercropped with garlic, of course), and wisely mulched with straw over Winter.

No, *forget mulching the garlic*, I tutted. Hard neck garlic loves frost. With a click of the mouse, the mulch was gone...

The program even showed me colourful three dimensional pictures of my garden at any moment in the year, viewed from the unlikeliest perspective.

Like the serpent in Eden

I could drag myself on my stomach, like the serpent in Eden, through rows of tomatoes as big as mountains. *Or* zoom up for a hawk's-eye view of the entire Croft - as prettily stitched together as a Gobelin tapestry.

How toil-free and enjoyable gardening is, viewed on a computer!

A mouse is your friend, not your foe. Viruses are zapped in moments. And the recycling bin never smells.

Vastly encouraged, I filled the garage with cloches for my early salad **Bed B**. I bought a trailer, wherewith to import manure for the 2.3 tonnes of potatoes that my program assured me I could grow in **Bed C**.

When the computer warned me I would need at least 3500 transplants over the year to fill the remaining 20 beds, I ordered a greenhouse for seed propagation.

Alas, it is a maxim of historians that no military plan survives its first contact with the enemy. Especially when the general in charge (me) has not even bothered to reconnoitre the territory.

My computer had lied

So when, optimistically festooned with computer printouts, I ventured into the paddock for my first serious inspection that Spring... I should not have been surprised to find that my computer had lied.

Frankly, I had inherited the worst soil this side of the Mongolian steppes.

I pushed in a trowel to get a soil sample, as textbooks advise. The trowel bent.

Only with a pick axe could I make a hole one foot deep. I found the top eight inches was hard clay plus large flints, compacted together by horses' hooves since the time of the Civil War.

Under it lay a solid three inch hardpan of chalk.

My soil was schizophrenic

The soil pH at the top was 6 - mildly acidic. Eight inches below, it was 7.5 - alkaline. My soil was schizophrenic. No wonder it was already showing evidence of plantain, dock and the pink sporulating fronds of marestail - all indicators of an acid soil. Yet everywhere too was fat hen (lamb's quarters), usually a sign of alkaline conditions.

In later months, every other invasive or perennial weed that has ever gibbered out of a gardener's nightmare came to haunt me. Thistle, bindweed, creeping buttercup, couch grass, ground elder, giant hogweed, dandelions plus, of course, nettles.

Only Japanese knotweed was absent, which rather disappointed me. The young shoots are delicious, cooked like asparagus.

Above all, I had marestail. *La belle dame sans merci...* To that grim lady, I shall return again.

Force 8 gales

In later months, I came to discover our paddock was the Most Favoured target of local force 8 gales. They would gust off the Chiltern hills, form a vortex in our valley, then drop upon us - howling. Even in high Summer.

They tumbled our cast iron bench over and again, as if it was matchwood. They tossed my cloches in the air like zeppelins and exploded the top out of the greenhouse.

No, there wasn't much left of the bean trellises, either.

But forgive me, I am getting ahead of myself...

A modest quiz

At this point, gentle reader, I ask your counsel. Given my awful soil, and a foolish insistence on growing vegetables there regardless, what would *you* have done?

1. Rotavated manure into the soil to break up the clay and improve the texture? **Yes/No**

2. Sprayed glyphosate weedkiller on every weed? **Yes/No**

3. Laid a thick plastic membrane across the field, then set transplants into holes cut in the membrane? **Yes/No**

4. Covered the paddock in six inches of wood chips? **Yes/No**

5. Swathed the field in old carpets for a year or two, to starve out the weeds - and abandoned all thoughts of growing in it meanwhile? **Yes/No**

6. Strimmed or mowed the weeds every week to weaken them so that eventually they'd give up? **Yes/No**

7. Built raised beds and filled them with 'perfect' soil?
Yes/No

8. Given up yourself - and moved house? **Yes/No**

Answers to this modest quiz

With the hindsight of experience, I can reply fairly to each question. Because I took *every* action suggested above - with the exception of moving house. (My wife had fallen too deeply in love with the Aga.)

1. Rotavate.

Many tons of manure did I rotavate in, to the unspeakable delight of every perennial weed. I simply chopped and proliferated their roots so, within weeks, ten weeds grew in the place of one.

Annual weeds loved it too. At last, their seeds - long asleep in the ground - felt the awakening kiss of light and air.

The rotavator also created a further little hard pan, around six inches beneath the surface. Now the roots of those plants I really wanted to grow would meet *two* barriers...

2. Spray glyphosate.

Normal weedkillers make no enduring impact on perennial weeds.

Fierce brushwood killers not only sterilise the soil but also render it too toxic to grow any vegetable safely there for many years.

Nor do they always work, I found, against brambles... or marestail.

Glyphosate is claimed to kill almost all weeds, even marestail, yet degrade at once on contact with the soil. So within a few weeks, vegetables can safely be sown there.

In my experience, it's just not true - on two counts.

A. To kill marestail reliably with any strong weedkiller, you have to first rub its leaves vigorously to crack their scaly coating. This is simply not practical if you have a quarter acre of marestail.

B. Glyphosate is a fiercely poisonous chemical.

Trials found that, 90 days after spraying it, half of the toxic compounds had still not degraded in the soil.

I merely report *The Journal of Pesticide Reform* 15(3), 1995.

Truly, I cannot say whether glyphosate is safe or not. Only that I felt deeply uneasy when, in the first year and in utter despair, I did spray it on the paddock - thrice.

Marestail was only patchily suppressed. And next year, all the other weeds came back anyway. So, if you go this route, it's Tumbleweed forever and you can forget about organic gardening.

Incidentally, US growers are now finding that marestail, if much sprayed by glyphosate, becomes resistant to it. As will, no doubt, all weeds in time...

3. Lay a plastic membrane.

At first glance, laying tough plastic sheet over the entire field seems like a relatively cheap and foolproof solution. Indeed, I did exactly that in Janice's flower pot garden and nary a weed poked its head back for three years.

But I wanted to grow in the soil, not in tubs or growbags above it. (I could do that on my patio.) Of course, that entails cutting flaps in the plastic to get the plants in. Not to mention watering them.

Out pop weeds

Once you cut holes, *out pop weeds*.

Plus... every year, you must remove the plastic to refresh the soil with manure or compost, give it a thorough soaking, then replace the plastic. That's only feasible in small beds.

When I tried plastic on a small part of the paddock, I found it impossible to dig planting holes into my hard soil - through the plastic.

> Of course, the YeoPod method might have made it child's play. In those innocent days, however, I had not yet discovered YeoPods.

As a weed suppressant, tough *impermeable* plastic is unbeatable.

But you had better start with fertile, friable soil. And if you have a *really* bad weed problem, permeable plastic - which lets in moisture - won't suppress bindweed, dock or marestail at all, I found, even if weighted down with heavy planks. Too much light filters through.

The plastic will rise inexorably - and the planks will dance like little oil rigs two foot in the air, atop struts of triumphant weeds.

4. Cover with woodbark.

This absurdly expensive, though decorative, mulch did work for me - for 18 months. For two seasons, I was able to grow through the bark, using many of the tactics I will share with you later.

Six inches of sawdust, pine needles or fresh wood shavings might also have suppressed even marestail for a season (though, as we'll see later, woody materials should never be mixed *into* the soil unless the soil has been well manured first).

I've no doubt the rotting wood made my soil even more acidic.

True, I should have scattered lime on the surface beforehand.

Every year or so, I found, you must also *renew* wood bark - or indeed any organic mulch.

As I didn't own a sawmill (or a bank), wood chips proved to be merely a quick fix. And a futile option.

5. Swathe the field in old carpet.

This option is even cheaper than plastic membrane if you cultivate a few friendly carpet fitters. They have to pay anyway to dispose of their offcuts as 'trade waste' so will gladly drive them to your door. Free.

On a separate plot where the soil was already cultivated and friable, I had great fun laying a carpet bed, cutting flaps in it and growing broccoli. The carpet rendered it immune to cabbage root fly.

In Winter, I simply rolled up the carpet and refreshed the soil, and in Spring I rolled the carpet back.

Carpet made from synthetic fibres lasted me at least three years outdoors. (Then I had the joy of disposing of it...)

But, I tell you truly, carving holes in carpet laid on soil is *hard work*. It blunts a carpet knife in moments. On large areas, the sheets must be very well overlapped or... bindweed, dock and buttercup will simply crawl around the edges.

Even though you keep carpet on the soil for a decade, hoping to kill everything, you won't kill marestail. The moment you take it off, back it comes.

> A landscape gardener told me he had once knocked down a Victorian wall. Within weeks, precisely where the old wall had stood, marestail was everywhere - but it had not existed in the garden in living memory. Nor

could it be seen anywhere else.

Was this the 'edge' effect, the well-known principle that the rims of landslides and other disturbed soil areas are spectacularly fertile?

"No," my friend averred. "That marestail had been under the bricks for 150 years, *just waiting its moment*."

So what chance does an old carpet have?

6. Mow the weeds every week.

If you cut even the toughest perennials back for long enough, their roots become exhausted and they die, 'tis said. So I bought an electric strimmer.

Foolish me. It took 24 hours to recharge its battery then worked for just 15 minutes before having to be recharged. A child's toy.

I traded it in quickly for a heavy-duty petrol strimmer.

Bliss! On one tankful of petrol, it strimmed at least 1000 sq foot of tangled undergrowth, sprayed my goggles with muck and chopped tough saplings and brambles into mulch. My only complaint was the plastic string had to be manually replaced every ten minutes.

> Tapping the end on the ground did *not* helpfully shoot out new string, as the manual claimed. Has that trick worked, *ever...* for *anyone*?

Strimming a quarter acre takes around three hours, I found, allowing for petrol refills, cleaning one's goggles and replacing the string. *Plus* one hour at the outset - to get the engine started.

When the weeds grew back, I borrowed my wife's petrol mower. It coped well with the toughest weeds, as it should.

(Previously, I had used it to macerate twigs and kitchen waste for the compost bin. I had just piled them on the patio and run the mower through them on its lowest setting. Of course, I hadn't told Janice that.)

Then... Disaster!

A large flint flew back, struck me under the chin, rendered me unconscious for several minutes and severed an artery.

Luton & Dunstable hospital put in nine stitches and said - if my wife had not broken every speed limit between Ivinghoe and Luton to get me there - I'd be dead.

> "If I'd known that," she muttered "I wouldn't have driven through that ruddy red light."

Janice then took back her mower and sternly forbade me from using it again - on either kitchen waste, weeds or grass.

> Chuckle... Has any man ever found a more cunning way - to avoid mowing the lawn?

Undoubtedly, mowing weeds forever, works. But I wanted to grow vegetables *now* and not in a decade's time - having meanwhile exhausted my wife's patience plus a refinery-full of petrol.

7. Build raised beds.

In despair, I raided our little daughter's college fund and hired a contractor to cover the paddock with eight vast raised beds, 14 inches high - a total of 960 sq foot.

> He filled each with a perfect mix of sifted topsoil and compost, having an ideally neutral pH of 7.

My wife protested "what of our daughter's education?". I thundered "Education? What is that, woman, *compared with propagation?*" (Still, she made me pay it all back.)

Now I had virgin weed-free soil. I could grow anything!

I felt newly empowered...

In late Spring, I sauntered into the garden to erect trellises on the raised beds and what should I find? In every one, a mattress of **M*******!**

I had forgotten that unprintable weed spreads, not only by roots, *but also from windblown spores.*

Soilwise, I was back to square one. Newly impoverished...

Raised beds?

If my problem had been merely hopeless soil, raised beds would have solved it admirably. At a price.

Even if the soil had been mildly contaminated, eg. with heavy metals or chemical run off, I could still have laid a tough membrane on it before filling the beds, and grown vegetables on top of it - in reasonable safety.

If my weed problem had been restricted to thistles, dock or dandelions, I might simply have chopped them down and eaten them.

> Peeled and pickled thistle stems make a delightful salad, dandelion roots can be roasted like parsnips or turned into coffee, and I can give you delicious recipes for dock - and dock seed too.

I'd then have piled salt on the stumps. They wouldn't have come back.

I'd have welcomed other weeds

Comfrey, chickweed and nettles?

If I didn't have them, I'd have had to grow them. *To eat them!* And to infuse into nutrient-rich plant foods. (See Chapter 16.)

Bindweed? Tackle it early, and it's *not* invasive. Pull it enough and it gives up. Meanwhile, I could have used the bindweed tendrils as string - to lash beans and peas to my trellises. Once the vines had found their way, the dead tendrils would have dropped off.

Buttercup, rosebay willow herb and vetch? They'd have gone in Janice's flower vase.

> Steamed rosebay leaves and young vetch pods are also edible, I've proven, if mixed with other greens. But only if you're famished...

Most weeds have *some* use. Except marestail.

No, I lie.

Marestail makes a splendid fungicidal foliar spray, shampoo and herbal medicine. Rabbits thrive on it.

It is also the Mother of Invention.

Why? It directly lead me to the discovery of the greatest horticultural advance since Jethro Tull perfected the plow.

He did it for all the wrong reasons, of course. He thought that soil must be pulverised by a plow so that plant roots, possessing little 'mouths', could more easily eat it. In that, he was wrong.

Yet the world has blessed him since.

Modesty prevents my comparing myself to Mr Tull. So I will now merely outline for you the stunning principle of the YeoPod, so simple yet so versatile.

And I will let *you* be the judge...

Chapter 2

The subtle beauty of the YeoPod

Many and cunning were the ways that I grew vegetables galore in my paddock, in those early years, despite impossible soil and weeds.

I chronicled them in my prior book *The Lazy Kitchen Gardener* (Village Guild).

But that was the era of innocence, before I discovered the YeoPod.

To understand the subtle beauty of the Yeopod I must take you back several years to when wood chip swathed the Croft and my most pestilential weeds were, for a while, subdued.

That year, I faced the task of growing, outdoors, 30 different varieties of rare heirloom tomatoes so I could share the seed with members of the Village Guild.

> This is a most excellent gardening society, with members in six continents, whereof you will read in the Appendix. You *will*, won't you?

That meant setting out some 120 transplants.

I was loathe to...

blunt my pickaxe, bend my spade and break my back digging 120 planting 'pockets' in that rock-hard soil, each of one cubic foot, then filling them with compost and good topsoil.

Besides, I didn't have to hand 3000 litres of either.

Nor - on ethical principles alone - would I blanket the paddock with 60 tomato GrowBags, packed with peat and chemical fertiliser, bought with shame from a garden centre.

Tomatoes *never* achieve their full potential in a shallow purchased GrowBag anyway. And these tomatoes were supposed to be *organically* grown!

The answer?

Several glasses of elderflower lemonade.

At least, they gave me the answer. I leapt in the air. I waved my arms. I cried "Eureka!".

At once, Mycroft went into premature hibernation. Mycroft is our tortoise, and very wise.

I rushed into the paddock with a crowbar and mallet.

I hammered the crowbar into the soil 12 inches deep, straight through the wood chip, flints and hardpan.

Fortified with elderflower lemonade, I found this surprisingly easy.

I whacked the top of the crowbar back and forth till I had a GrowCone some eight inches wide at the top and a foot deep. I hoped this might allow the plants to get their taproots through the hardpan. It would also provide a water reservoir.

I filled the cone with an artful mix of wilted comfrey, powdered eggshells, sand, topsoil and homemade compost. The perfect starter soil for tomatoes, I imagined.

I was wrong. *I had omitted the book matches and fish heads.* But this was my first experience in custom-making a potting mix and I later learned better formulations. See Chapter 13.

I banged in the crowbar again...

beside the cone and thrust a cane into that hole. I watered the cone lavishly and set a tomato rootball in the top three inches of each cone. Then I pushed the wood chip back around the tomato stem, to suppress weed growth and conserve moisture.

Apart from subsequent watering, that's *all* I did.

And 120 tomato plants grew bountifully to yield me enough seed for several years.

When I cut off the dead plants in October I left their roots in the soil to provide a friable, well drained planting pocket in which I might grow a different crop *next* year.

I calculated...

if I assiduously sank GrowCones all around the paddock for five years, my problem soil - enriched by potting mix and root residues, and with its hardpan broken up - would be transformed.

Each GrowCone took me only some three minutes to make and plant out, with all components to hand. For 120 plants, that was still a day's labour, of course.

But a crowbar is less work than a spade.

Had I dug conventional planting pockets, each of one cubic foot, the task would (I found, after digging one) have taken eight times longer. Or rather, *no time at all* - because I wouldn't even have attempted it.

Moreover, each cone used far less potting mix than a planting pocket.

So easy was the process that...

I set out some runner bean transplants in GrowCones too - accompanied by tall canes - and, for the first time in the paddock, got six foot vines.

That's not impressive, I agree. But previously, every runner bean I'd sunk into that awful soil had turned into a dwarf bean.

For my birthday, my wife bought me 200 onion sets. (Janice loves onions.) Undeterred, I rammed GrowCones all over the paddock, set an onion bulb in each and... Lo! we had 200 onions.

I then decided to make an **Instant Forest Garden**, an edible mini-Paradise - using GrowCone technology. So magnificently did this bloom that it inspired an entire Chapter of this book (see Chapter 4).

Yet evidently, GrowCones were only a partial solution.

For example, my indeterminate tomatoes - that should have needed stopping after four trusses lest they grow forever - stopped themselves when just three feet tall.

So prolific are Abraham Lincoln beefsteak tomatoes that each plant *should* have yielded 5-10lb of fruit and demanded a cage to support them. But 2lb in total weight was the best crop any beefsteak plant gave me.

Obviously, the plants had become rootbound in the cones. They needed to expand their roots - *laterally*.

Thus, was the YeoPod born.

Suppose, I wondered, I set a large plastic flower pot on top of each cone? Upside down, and with its base removed? *And* I filled the pot with the same custom-made potting mix - and set the transplant in the top?

Its roots could then expand laterally, an important requirement for almost every plant, especially tomatoes. The tap root might also enjoy as much as 16 inches of depth, enough to gratify even sweet corn and sunflowers, I thought.

In all but the hardest compacted soils, the taproot would

also extend *laterally* into the
surrounding soil - and have access to
further trace minerals, nutrients and
moisture.

An upside down flower pot

An upside down flower pot was clearly
what the world had been waiting for.

> I had always wondered why flower
> pots are made with the *smallest*
> soil area at the bottom, where the
> roots most need to expand, and
> the *widest* soil mass at the top -
> where the plant can't use it
> anyway.
>
> And why a flower pot has a base so narrow it
> encourages the wretched thing to fall over at the
> slightest breath and scatter its contents.
>
> And why, when we tap out the rootball, the top-heavy
> pot design encourages the potting mix to disintegrate
> around our feet. To the unspeakable distress of the
> plant...
>
> I had concluded the flower pot was so absurdly
> designed, it was clearly a conspiracy between pot
> manufacturers and compost vendors *to promote
> excessive purchases of compost.*

Further YeoPod joys presented themselves...

The soil in the top collar would be a natural **mulch**,
conserving water and suppressing weeds, I reasoned.

Watering would be a snap.

A hose or watering can could direct water into every collar with no wastage. That would be important in the event of a hosepipe ban when I might have to ferry water 50 yards to the plants in a watering can.

Drainage would take care of itself. Even if the cone had been rammed into hard clay, and it became saturated in a downpour, enough drainage should still occur at surface level to keep the plant oxygenated and healthy.

The collars would also **protect** young plants from wind damage in the early days, if I set them a few inches below the rim.

Indeed, plants that benefit from a little **earthing up**, like celery and leeks, might be set half way down the collar - and the collar topped up with soil as they grew. No more digging trenches!

Each collar might also become a cloche...

for early transplants or March-sown broad beans and lettuces. I could drape fleece or clear perforated polythene over the top and secure it with tough industrial sellotape, then take it off when the plants were up.

Or I could protect brassica from butterflies and many other flying pests by pushing four canes into each corner of the collar at an angle, so they splayed out.

I might then push a cork onto each cane, drape fleece or fine mesh netting over the canes, and wire it to perforations in the rims.

'Twould be far less work than trying to erect a mighty

mesh cage over a conventional brassica bed - especially for one person in a high wind, unaided by a patient spouse.

The result would also look quite pretty, like a beekeeper's hat.

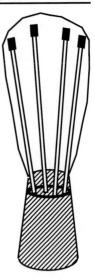

The plants raised above ground might have better **ventilation** and so be less subject to fungal diseases like botrytis and blight brought on by high humidity, I hoped.

> Oh, how I prayed to St Fiacre - the patron saint of gardeners - to safeguard my next year's tomatoes against blight!

Adjacent weeds would no longer be a threat.

The YeoPod plants would soar smugly above them, their roots and leaves uncrowded by competitors. If monster weeds *did* encroach, I reckoned it would be easy enough to pull, mow, scythe or strim them, with little fear of harming the YeoPod plant - protected in its collar.

Pest problems would be much reduced.

Snails were rampant in the paddock but, I'd already proven, they would *not* climb a collar smeared with a band of vaseline, sump oil, duck fat or used cooking oil mixed with salt or soot. Or a collar ringed with copper wire.

A tall collar might even give some protection against **flying pests** like carrot fly, which hug the ground.

Cabbage root fly and other **burrowing insects** could be repelled with a top mulch - a ring of cardboard or carpet within the collar. That mulch would also suppress any wind-blown weeds that tried to grow in the collar itself.

Mice and **voles** were unlikely to devastate legume seeds or root crops in YeoPods, I reasoned, as this would entail first burrowing down then... upwards. Rodents rarely have the college education to do that.

If moles, voles or mice *did* become a problem, I could simply sink the collars very *deep* - or lay ¼inch wire mesh at the base of each collar.

A YeoPod would also be relatively **cat** and **dog** proof. At least, young plants would not be scratched out or fouled.

> Not being blessed with poultry, however, I couldn't say whether YeoPod plants might survive a duck attack.

Rabbits, **birds** and **pheasants** would be far less likely to crop plants that began a foot above ground, or that were tucked well within a protective collar.

Bean and pea seeds, for example, might be set a few inches below a collar and the top covered with a square of netting or muslin secured by a tough rubber band. By the time the rubber perished, the netting could come off and the legumes would be tall enough to cope with the odd peck and nibble.

Harvesting and tending a raised YeoPod plant - as much as 18 inches above ground level - might also be easier for folk with **disabilities**, I concluded.

> As I have sundry back troubles, and sometimes can't bend at all, I found this a very welcome bonus.

In fact, the YeoPod appeared to offer virtually all the

benefits of a raised bed *without the cost or labour of constructing one.*

Its versatility was awe-inspiring.

I realised I *didn't* need to buy plastic flower pots. I could get endless supplies of big plastic tubs in a variety of shapes, from florists. *Free for the asking.* Often, they just threw them away.

> A tall slim tub might serve for plants that need root depth, like brassica and tomatoes. Squash would do well in a wide flat collar - perhaps a big pot sliced in half.

> Salad plants, marigolds and herbs could be grown in smaller collars, cut from large yogurt pots or ice cream tubs.

Many other creative sources for collars came to mind (see Chapter 6).

YeoPods gain altitude

Conceivably, a YeoPod might be built in two tiers - a wide shallow collar surmounted by a slim one.

In the top would go a tomato or brassica. Around it in the lower collar might be set spring onions, stubby carrots, chives, small beetroot, herbs, salad leaves or companion plants like tagetes.

All might do well as catch crops under a full grown tomato plant, I thought, despite its shading. And by the time a cabbage or other late maturing vegetable had grown large enough to swamp them, the catch crops would be ready to pull.

A tall wide collar also provides a natural base for a bean typee (I told myself).

Insert a tall cane to one side of the cone, within the collar. Punch holes around the collar rim. Lead string from the holes to the top of the cane. Grow climbing beans and peas up the strings.

I love my wife

Graciously, I vowed to make a little YeoPod trellis for my wife - who inexplicably likes inedible flowers like sweet peas.

However, in a YeoPod trellis, it would be wise to ram *several* cones together under each collar so each climber could sink its roots down into at least one... I determined.

In fact, the fertile possibilities offered by a YeoPod trellis provoked many a happy experiment. (See Chapter 9)

The future of horticulture

The more I looked into YeoPods, the more convinced I became that they were the future of horticulture.

They spelled the end of rotavators as we know them. They empowered the little man (and woman) to make a stand against the conspiracy of weedkiller firms, the fatuity of 'coffee table' gardening books - and the tyranny of flower pot designers.

But first I had to show the world, how to use them. So gentle reader, let me start here...

The basic YeoPod process

I assume that you have very unpromising soil - a bed of builder's rubble, a long-neglected allotment, a reclaimed city lot or a Mongolian steppe.

In the unlikely case that your soil is totally weed-free, YeoPods will *still* bring you many benefits, as we've explored.

But in that case you may, with my forgiveness, omit the first step here.

1. Strim or scythe off the weeds. Leave their roots in place to add to the soil texture.

True, perennial weeds will grow back. But YeoPods laugh at perennial weeds.

2. Using a mallet, ram a hole in the soil with a crowbar, long metal dibber or a sharpened broom handle - at least 12 inches deep and as deep as you can conveniently achieve.

3. Widen the hole by whacking the crowbar around, or by inserting a pointed wooden stake like a sharpened hoe handle and wiggling it around, to form a cone around 6 - 8 inches wide at the top.

4. If the cone fills in as soon as you remove the stake, because the soil is dry or sandy, pour several pints of water into the cone. Then repeat step 3.

5. Fill the cone with purchased compost or - better still - your own potting mix, compounded according to the plant you intend to grow. (See Chapter 13)

6. Ram another deep hole beside the cone but, this time, don't wiggle it. Push into that hole a cane, if the plant is a climber or will need support.

7. Water the cone lavishly. I mean, around two gallons - an entire watering can full!

> This will be the plant's water reservoir for weeks to come.

8. Put an upturned plastic pot over the cone, its base sliced off to form a collar.

9. Pour compost or potting mix into the collar, just enough so the first leaves of your intended transplant will show above the collar. Lay your transplant in that hole and pour compost, or potting mix, around the transplant to about one inch of the rim.

> If a transplant needs sheltering from wind, or earthing up, set it so the first leaves are a few inches *below* the rim.

10. Water the transplant well. Then keep watering it (and feeding, if necessary).

And, uh, *that's it...*

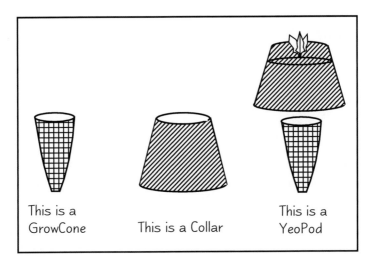

This is a
GrowCone

This is a Collar

This is a
YeoPod

Chapter 3

YeoPods rise to the Ultimate Test

Allow me to backtrack, to the year when my paddock was swathed in wood chip and the weeds had been suppressed, for a season.

Next year, back came the weeds, of course. *I welcomed them!*

Soon YeoPod technology would have them cowering in their beds, I thought.

That was just as well as... in that subsequent year, I had foolishly committed myself to growing *64* different varieties of rare heirloom tomatoes, their seeds collected from all over the world. That meant propagating, hardening off and setting out at least 220 plants.

At this point, I remembered I was the world's most slothful gardener. So I applied the **First Rule of Lazy Gardening**: get *other people* to do the work you don't like.

The First Rule in practice

In early May, I persuaded a retired friend that YeoPod gardening was scientifically proven to be better aerobic exercise than jogging. (I read it in a newspaper, so it must be true.) And cheaper than a health club.

Yay, I would even *pay* him a modest fee for the privilege of pioneering this horticultural triumph. One day he might join me on the platform at the Nobel Awards ceremony, I hinted.

He demurred at the fee.

I darkly reminded him that WWOOFers (Willing Workers On Organic Farms) would do it for nothing, just a bunkbed and

a ploughman's lunch. He told me, if I doubled the fee he'd
bring his own lunch, thank you.

So I doubled the fee.

He set to work with such amazing vigour...

that it exhausted me to watch him. In just two days, he
had rammed 256 GrowCones, filled them with an
assortment of potting mixes, topped them with collars,
invested each with a cane and transplant, and labelled them

"It's easy once you get into the rhythm of it," he
claimed.

I now had 256 YeoPods!

You will rightly despise me...

for paying someone else to do my gardening.

It violates the sacred canons of Self Reliance.

Indeed, I once wrote a book with that title, currently available at
Amazon (and priced far too cheaply, methinks). *But I digress...*

I should at least have paid him, not in cash, but with a
credit note exchangeable for 60lbs of heirloom tomatoes.
Shouldn't I?

But he was of that unreasonable breed who prefers *money*.

Besides, I used the time thus saved to write another
chapter for my book *The Lazy Kitchen Gardener*, without
which the mountains of Nepal might have been less fertile.

(It's a long story. See Chapter 8.)

No, I do *not* suggest you pay anyone to make YeoPods.

So quick and effortless are they, you can make a dozen
yourself - if all materials are to hand - in under an hour!

If you *must* make several hundred, you are probably running a farm and
can get an EC subsidy for your labourers (provided you promise to

throw away the vegetables they grow).

So inspired was I that I made eight more YeoPods for heirloom pumpkins. Each had to be of the same variety because all squash varieties cross-pollinate and I wanted to save pure seed.

I also planted two Patty Pan squash plants in YeoPods.

> I caged them in bags sewn from my wife's net curtains, lest insects devastate the purity of their seed - and that of the adjacent pumpkins. Do you know how *big* a bag must be, to cage a lusty squash?

Tomatoes are far less of a problem in this respect although beefsteak, potato leaf and currant varieties may also cross-pollinate to a tiny degree with each other.

This is just as well, as sewing 220 tomato cages - I determined - was a Challenge Too Far.

I also set out ten brussel sprouts, ten cabbages and ten broccoli plants in YeoPods - using the artful mixes you will find described in Chapter 13.

> In this, I was admirably selfless - as my family disdain all brassica not bought at Tesco. And I don't eat brassica much anyway.

All flourished so magnificently that I concluded... *YeoPods work!*

Chapter 4

The Instant (YeoPod) Forest Garden

I concede you may not need the full technology of the YeoPod to gain a bounteous harvest from your soil.

If you have been gracious enough to read *The Lazy Kitchen Gardener*, you will have warmed to my recipe therein for growing your own paradise Forest Garden in a mere five months, from sunflowers.

But did you ever suspect, that I owed it all - to *YeoPods*?

No? Just as well, because... I didn't.

Not really. These were, after all, early days. All I used to grow my Forest Garden, in the worst soil imaginable, were Grow*Cones* - the primitive precursors of YeoPods.

But they served well enough.

One May, I set out in the paddock no fewer than 142 giant sunflowers, germinated in toilet rolls.

> Loo rolls are superb for propagating most large seeds, like sunflowers and legumes. Even tubers and tomatoes. But they are a *total disaster* for brassica or lettuces.
>
> The reasons are complex.
>
> Fortunately, I have explored this issue separately - in some technical depth - in a humble monograph. This is available on request to all Village Guild members in good standing.
>
> When you join the Guild - or if you are already a member - simply contact me. Cry 'Loo rolls!'. *And I will oblige.*

Please forgive my digression. Let's return to the

sunflowers. The seedlings had been in the greenhouse for 42 days and were as lanky as walking stick onions.

GrowCones came to the rescue

Now that I had discovered the GrowCone method, however, each one took me mere seconds to plant.

I arranged the transplants decoratively like a forest, with a winding path through the middle. It lead to a central haven, big enough to host a deckchair and a case of beer.

I dreamt of being able - soon - to disappear like Dr Livingstone into a tropical jungle, dappled with butterflies and crowned by 12-inch flowerheads.

> Occasionally from the trees would emerge smoke signals of herbal tobacco, instructing Janice to bring me another case of beer.

> For sustenance, I sank two seeds of a climbing french bean beside each perimeter sunflower plant.

This proved to be a mistake.

The beans grew so fast that they throttled the sunflowers, and had to be sacrificed.

Incidentally, most plants grow perfectly well alongside sunflowers, provided all receive ample water. Sunflowers have gained their reputation for being *allelopathic* (poisonous) to adjacent plants largely, I suspect, because they dehydrate them.

> The following year, I took care *not* to sow beans beside sunflowers, until the sunflowers were already four foot tall.

Lo, my Instant Forest Garden was a triumph!

Throughout August I sat within it, like a bug in an apple, invisible to all yet irrefutably diligent with my laptop computer and cordless phone.

In October, the sunflowers yielded me enough sturdy canes to make three ten-foot bean trellises, enough seeds to feed every wild bird in the county plus enough woody rootballs - when mixed with fresh horse manure to rot them down - to build a fertile 24 cubic foot raised bed.

The weaker canes were shredded into mulch, and laid around my YeoPods the following year to suppress adjacent weeds.

Moreover, pulling out the roots gave me... *142 ready-made planting holes!*

> The sunflower roots had broken up the hard pan, all by themselves.

Next year, I found those holes unspeakably helpful - when the time came to plant, in the paddock, *my 220-plus heirloom tomatoes.*

Chapter 5

Clever tools for the YeoPod professional

As you will have seen, the lusty YeoPod gardener can look forward to a lifetime of adventure.

Here are just a few of the clever possibilities that make YeoPods as versatile in the garden as, well, a Swiss Army knife.

> Why don't they market those lovely multi-purpose gadgets for gardeners? Then they could be called Swiss *Land* Army knives...

Mulches

If your weeds are like marestail, thistles or bindweed - fierce enough to grow up and through a ten inch collar, despite its formidable soil barrier - you can mulch the *base* of the collar.

For example, fill the GrowCone then lay over it a square of thick manure bag plastic with a two inch diameter hole in the centre.

> Do *not* use plastic supermarket bags. They are designed to degrade quickly. But thick plastic bags from quality shops should last forever.

The swelling roots from the collar-grown plant will readily find their way through the hole and *down* into the GrowCone for moisture and nutrients. But few weeds will find that elusive hole - and grow *up* through it.

Even a degradeable barrier...

cut from old curtain, cardboard, a thick woollen shirt, or several sheets of newspaper - likewise perforated in the centre - will suppress vigorous weeds for a season, if firmly held down by the soil above.

Another tip: When you cut off the bases of the plastic flower pots, keep them handy.

Five or six of them can be overlapped in a circle at the bottom of a collar, leaving a gap in the middle. These will suppress not only weeds within the collar but also weeds around it.

To prevent annual weeds becoming a nuisance in the top of the collar (though they rarely do harm), lay there an inch or so of sand or sterilised purchased compost.

Any impermeable barrier will serve as well, of course.

A wad of old nylon socks is impregnable - and immortal.

It will also stop flying insects laying grubs.

Those aesthetically inclined might craft cones out of thick coloured cardboard, wrap them around the plant stem and tape them together with industrial strength sellotape.

Coloured cone mulches offer no advantage whatsoever over flat mulches, but they look scientific - and will awe your neighbours.

Scientific? Coloured mulches do have their advocates. See Chapter 7.

The simplest way to suppress adjacent weeds...

is to set the YeoPods next to each other in double rows.

Indeed, if your collars are rectangular rather than round, they'll entirely cover the ground. Your grateful plants will then be assailed by weeds on only one side.

> Not that weeds can do much harm to a plant safely cordoned in a YeoPod.

Incidentally, you'll find it's a mistake to set out YeoPods more than four rows abreast. You'll never be able to reach into the inner rows.

To harvest your crops, you will have to hire a crane, a small child and a bungee rope.

Cloches

The YeoPod collar provides a firm base for every kind of impromptu cloche.

Four canes can be inserted at each corner of the collar, their tops made safe from your eyes with corks, small plastic cola bottles or beer cans.

Over these can be draped large clear plastic bags, such as the kind used by dry cleaners.

Do perforate them or the plants, in hot weather, will be steam-cleaned.

Unbreakable clear bags can be bought cheaply from building supply centres which sell them as rubble bags. When their mission as cloches has been fulfilled, recycle them into comfrey tea pots, solar stills or home made Grow Bags.

Penetrating light will not harm any plants grown in clear GrowBags as their roots will be exposed only at the *under* surface, where the sun don't shine.

The soil at the sides may simply develop an interesting veneer of green algae.

Tie a heavy stone...

A simple way to hold the bags down, more convenient than string or tape, is to tie a heavy stone in each of four corners, gathering the corners into pockets which enwrap the stone. The bags will stay down in all but the heaviest wind.

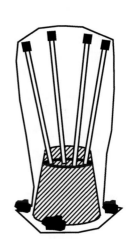

They can also be easily slipped off on hot days.

YeoPods also make it simple to erect isolation cages if you're growing plants that need protection from cross-pollination by insects, so their seeds can be saved true to the variety.

Drape over those canes in the same fashion a cloche or cylinder made from muslin or horticultural fleece.

An easy way to make a fleece cylinder

If your spouse wisely denies you access to the sewing machine, an easy way to make a cylinder is to cut a large square of fleece or net curtain.

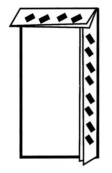

Fold it in half. Fold the top and side down an inch, and again, several times. And staple those folds secure with a heavy duty stapler.

Ordinary office staples tear out in moments.

Or just lace the folds in place with wire.

An isolation cage must be secured permanently at the base of the collar, eg. with strong tape, to exclude all insects. And it *must* stay in place all season long.

So, thankfully, you won't have to remove it too often.

> Okay, I *will* allow you to cut a little flap in the side to get your hose pipe in, but be sure to clip it back very securely with three clothes pegs.
>
> (If your spouse truculently denies you access to the clothes pegs, bulldog clips will suffice.)

A cage made from fleece or fine meshed netting will also protect plants from birds and caterpillars.

Not least, if you're brave enough to grow endive or dandelions, a cage made from *dark* cloth - even an old shirt, tied at the neck and armpits - will blanch them for you.

In this manner, a YeoPod might helpfully double as... a *scarecrow!*

> I cannot answer for chicory or radicchio, blanched in this way, because I find their taste so revolting I have never grown them.

A cage will keep insects off flowering runner beans, too.

Have you ever tried *dwarfing* a runner bean?

Just cut its tendrils when four foot high. Then twine them back on each other. They suppress weeds, and you'll still get a lot of beans - and you *won't* need a trellis.

Moreover, you can now *cage* those dwarfed beans - easily - against cross-pollination by insects.

This is important if you're trying to save the seed - pure - from rare heirloom runners, yet the official isolation distance for pure seed is a half-mile or more.

This way, you can get and save pure seed from runners, year on year - yet it's painless. *Not many people know this....*

A *moveable feast*

If you grow tender perennials like swiss chard and runner beans, you could try moving them indoors in Winter then replanting them in Summer.

The trick is to make a GrowCone in the usual way. Then insert a nylon mesh bag in the collar before filling it with potting mix. Make sure the bag drapes over the top of the collar.

Supermarkets sell a variety of mesh bags, with vegetables included in them free.

When Winter frosts threaten, hold the bag tightly at the top and slip off the collar. The lower roots will then pull out of the GrowCone and you can insert the collar in a tray of damp sand indoors, overWinter.

One Village Guild member says she has kept the same runner bean *(Phaseolus coccineus)* plants alive for five years, using a similar method.

This idea *should* also work with French beans *(P. vulgaris)* which are perennials in South America. But has anybody ever tried it?

Try this method also with biennials like carrots and onions, if they're rare varieties and you want to replant them the following year to collect their seed.

Another way to protect perennial but tender plants in Winter...

is to leave them in the collar outdoors - and mulch it under a pile of leaves or straw, held down by a weighted hessian (burlap) sack.

The YeoTrellis

For a mighty plant like a beefsteak tomato, ram four canes deeply in each corner of the collar and make a cage by tying string or wire around it at eight inch intervals. As the plant grows, it will still sprawl out of its cage.

But you now have a structure

Keep tying the stems back to it, using pantyhose or spindled strips cut from old nylon socks - to avoid abraiding the stems.

For climbing vine-like plants like legumes, outdoor cucumbers, potatoes or achocha, simply ram *one* tall cane into the collar before you fill it.

If you grow climbing beans, you can pack at least three or four of them into one YeoPod, depending on the collar width. Or perhaps six peas.

Still, a single cane usually suffices.

That said, one year I grew Telephone Pole peas.

Have you ever seen a pea pod that's eight inches long? On vines ten foot tall?

I won't even mention Coon (Rose) Beans, each pod of which is as fat as a cucumber. Or Bean Peas, so big they make broad beans look like petit pois and yet are still, verifiably, peas.

For such gargantua, one cane thrust fecklessly into flimsy soil will *not* suffice.

Solution: set your YeoPods tightly together, two rows abreast. Sink the tallest canes you have, six foot long at

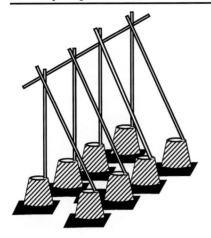

very least, one into each collar. And tie them together at the tops, with a further cane across the top, in a conventional trellis arrangement.

If you suffer Force 8 gales, as we do, I'd also suggest you lash the end of each trellis to the ground with sturdy flyropes. And further hold them down with flyropes, front and back.

This may seem Over the Top, in the halcyon wind-free climes of June. That's when - in the UK - you might typically plant out your beans.

Just let me say, when a hurricane last blew my bean trellises into three counties... it was *High Summer*.

Tie them down!

Other useful forms of trellis or typee...

can be made by inserting four canes in a large pod, splayed outward.

The climbing beans or peas, or whatever, will then hang from the canes within easy reach. Nor do the vines congest at the tips.

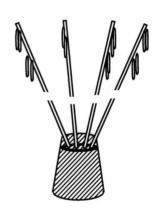

A variation is to ram a strong stave into the centre of a pod with a crosspiece at the top.

From those batons you can run strings down to the rim of the pod.

In this case, you would need to sink *four* cones below the pod - so the plants can get their roots down around the edge of the pod instead of through the centre.

For vining plants that need depth, you could even construct a *double* pod with the upper pod resting on the lower pod the conventional way up.

Four canes can then be thrust into this structure, and splayed out as before.

A YeoPod Hammock

Just as sturdy is a typee, made by setting four to six YeoPods together, with canes in situ.

Tie the canes together at the top.

You can also train melons and large squash - grown in YeoPods - along a *horizontal* trellis or hammock.

Bang in a sturdy wooden stave, around three foot long, against the side of the collar. Bang in another two staves, around four foot long, some four feet away.

These must be strong staves, and deeply buried. They'll need to take a *lot* of weight.

Tie strong netting - or rope - from the shorter stave up to the longer staves to give a crude hammock. As the melons or squash grow, twine them along the hammock.

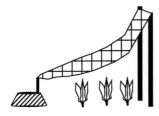

Its shade will itself suppress most weeds.

But in the earlier days, you could cleverly grow lettuces *under* the hammock. In tiny YeoPods, made from upended yogurt pots...

For utterly compacted soils

If your clay soil is so dense it can be rolled into Neolithic beakers, and then fired in a potter's kiln, perhaps a meagre crowbar will not suffice.

So I suggest here a solution: **a metal post holder.**

You can buy such fluted thugs, quite cheaply.

First, ram in a hole - 12 inch *deep*, or as *deep* as you can manage - with a crow bar or other sturdy pointed stave.

Then insert a metal post holder.

Hammer it down. Twist it. Batter it from all sides with your mallet.

Why? It will create a vast cone, with fluted side corridors.

A vast cone

When you sink in a transplant, that hungry plant will now have even more opportunities to expand its roots - sideways.

If it can't penetrate its roots beyond its GrowCone prison, no matter. It will *still* get ample nutrients.

If it can (and usually it can), it will be still further gratified.

A YeoPod - mightily expanded with a post holder - should be capable of growing, within itself, *any edible plant on this planet.*

Every YeoPod professional should have a metal post holder in their kitbag.

A YeoPod Pagoda

Is there any edible plant that *cannot* be grown in a YeoPod?

It's hard to think of one, though bananas or bread fruit would need a YeoPod as big as a barrel (see Chapter 6).

Cereal crops would be somewhat pointless, though grain amaranth might do well - and prove very useful for those who cannot eat gluten.

Even rhubarb would benefit from a large YeoPod.

Though it grows in almost any mildly acidic soil, it likes a lot of muck or liquid potash feed - which is easily introduced to a YeoPod.

Its massive roots would also help break up the adjacent soil.

Potatoes?

Easily done! But you'll need a **YeoPod Pagoda.**

Ram a large GrowCone with a metal post holder. Fill it with the special formulation you'll find in Chapter 13.

Push in four five foot canes and insert over them the largest collar you can find.

But this time, place it like a conventional flower pot - with its widest end *uppermost.*

Fill with more special potting mix.

Insert three chitted potatoes and cover them with some three inches of potting mix (or one of the formulations in

Chapter 13)..

When the leaves grow some two inches tall, drop another bottomless collar of the same size over those four canes.

Again, it should have its wide end at the top.

Add two inches of potting mix. (Etc.)

As the foliage grows, keep earthing it up - always leaving the very tops of the leaves visible. Finally, add a third collar (wide end at the top) and earth up the haulm again.

You'll now have a YeoPod Pagoda around three foot tall. Don't make it much taller or it will become unstable.

The point of stacking the collars with their *wide* end uppermost is that you can water *every layer* of the pagoda through the gaps around the base of each layer. If you want a decent crop, water each layer lavishly!

I think this tip is very original...

and I will pause before proceeding so you can applaud me.

Enough! *I will now proceed...*

When you want to harvest the potatoes, pull out the canes. And knock the pagoda over.

I'm sure you'll point out that a potato tub or 'barrel' can be made, with less fuss, from a large perforated manure bag and earthed up in the same way.

But will it give the same yield?

It's difficult to get enough water to the base of a barrel, where the potato roots are, by topwatering alone. But with a YeoPod Pagoda, you can easily direct the water where it's needed. To the roots.

The ultimate strawberry barrel

Of course, a YeoPod Pagoda also makes the ultimate

strawberry barrel.

The biggest reason that conventional strawberry barrels fail is that the plants, tucked into holes in the side, simply don't get enough water. Instead, it's easy to build a YeoPod Pagoda, cut holes in the side and tuck in the rootballs.

You can then water every tier of the pagoda, confident in the knowledge that ample water is getting immediately to every rootball.

And why stop with strawberries?

Herbs and trailing flowers are another option. Or perhaps strawberries interspersed with lobelia or small nasturtiums?

Flower afficionados will doubtless think of countless other combinations. I confess, if I can't *eat* a flower, I don't grow it...

How to grow Alphabetical Carrots

And here's an outrageous suggestion.

Why not cut many holes in the pagoda sides and... tuck in transplants of short-rooted carrots?

You will then have a **Carrot Tree.**

Yes, you *can* transplant carrots successfully, and other tubers too - if you germinate them in loo rolls and plant them out still within the loo rolls. Or, better, use Rootrainers.

I've been doing both for five years.

The only problem I find with growing carrots *laterally* is, the carrots grow in a Z or C shape.

The root goes down, the top goes up and the bit in the middle becomes confused.

If you grow two carrots closely together, they intertwine and become a B shape.

But alphabetical carrots still taste fine.

Of course, you could grow a **Salad Tree** too. Tuck in transplants of small lettuces, pak choi or other salad leaves. Intersperse them with tumbler tomatoes. Or almost any small vegetable or fruit.

Again, side watering is easy.

You could even tuck in some trailing flowers in the rims between the collars and have, verily, your own *little Hanging Gardens of Babylon.*

Put in the top a plant that needs a *long* taproot- like an exhibition carrot or parsnip, even a brussel sprout - and you have a complete vegetarian menu.

If you build a *very* wide YeoPod Pagoda, of course, you may want to bring supplementary water down through the middle.

This should not be necessary but, I concede, a central water reservoir *does* help in a drought. It also means, you don't need to water so often.

A central watering pipe

An easy way to do that is to take several plastic cola bottles, cut off their base, remove all the caps and ram them into each other.

Tape them into a tube with weather-proof industrial or gardening sellotape.

Screw the cap back on the lowest bottle.

Perforate the sides, just a few perforations towards the bottom and progressively more perforations towards the top.

This is very important, to ensure equal water distribution at every level. Other gardening textbooks *do not tell you this.*

In a drought, one member filled half her bottle with sand. This made the water seep out very *slowly,* she said.

I cannot attest to the value of this.

Sink the tube in the centre of the pagoda.

When you fill the tube with water, it will now seep out steadily at every level of the tube.

This tube can also be inserted in conventional strawberry barrels and (all else being equal) make the silly things actually work...

A tube carefully made like this should last you forever.

Well, *mine* are into their sixth year

A Double YeoPod

Some plants need a lot of root depth.
Brassica grown in the UK are notorious for sinking their roots to Australia, sampling the beer and hastily returning home.

For potholers like these, you can make a **Double Pot.**

Ram a conventional GrowCone but put on top of it a collar with its wide end uppermost. Fill with potting mix.

Place on top another but smaller collar, this time upturned - with its narrow end uppermost. Fill with potting mix.

Water can be introduced to the plant at both the top and the sides.

When you set your transplant or seed into the top collar, it will have almost three foot of depth to get its roots into.

Not to mention further space for lateral root growth at the base.

No garden vegetable needs more than that.

So perhaps we can *indeed* grow breadfruit in a YeoPod, after all?

When your 'soil' is concrete

One member told me his soil was pure clay and concrete. He couldn't even get a pickaxe into it. Could YeoPods still offer a solution?

Of course!

Simply set out Grow*Bags* on top of the soil. But conventional bags are useless if you want magnificent yields - there's not enough root depth.

Instead, make fat GrowBags out of plastic manure sacks or, at worst, black plastic garbage bags.

They usually survive one season outdoors before degrading.

Then place one or two YeoPod collars *over* each bag, with a hole cut underneath each one.

The plants would then have some room for root expansion, vertically into the bag as well as laterally into the collar.

At season's end, he could remove the collars if necessary, put a cloche over the bags and grow overWintering salad crops in them. They'll retain enough nutrients to sustain light-feeding plants another few months.

Questions I knew you'd ask

1. Are potatoes really a vine plant?

Yes. They'd be far happier climbing up a trellis than sulking in the ground. Professional potato breeders routinely train their potatoes up trellises.

Trouble is, you then have to treat them like melons. And truss each tuber (sorry, fruit) in a little bag. Opaque, of course, so the potato doesn't grow green and poisonous.

Frankly, it's a lot of work.

So can we *please* go back to growing potatoes underground? *Thank you...*

2. What's achocha?

It's pronounced 'ash-ooooo -sha!' like a long sneeze. It's one of the Lost Crops of the Incas and incredibly rare.

It yields three-inch green fruits just like gherkins, which - when young - you can stir-fry or slice into salads. When old, they can be stuffed and baked like green peppers.

It grows outdoors, even in the UK and the worst soil. And within eight weeks it rambles 15 foot high - across everything. It's the world's fastest-growing - edible - greenhouse shade plant.

Provided you grow it *outside* the greenhouse. Inside, it will choke *everything*.

Where can you get it in the UK? Simply join the Village Guild., ask me for it - and it's yours free!

(Sorry for the unsolicited commercial...)

3. Why might I want to make a solar still?

Pour undrinkable dregs of home made wine in the centre tray and you can tap off high proof alcohol in the outer tray.

Infuse *Tagetes minuta* flowers (Mexican marigold) - or the flowers of *any* aromatic companion plant - in that alcohol for a few weeks then spray it on any plants susceptible to flying pests.

I learned this from a scientific journal so it can't be wrong.

I have not tested the solar still since my reckless youth because distilling alcohol at home is illegal in the UK... of course.

However, you could always make herb essences using *supermarket vodka*, which has no other beneficial use but *is* legal...

Alas, a solar still works well only in continual, very hot weather.

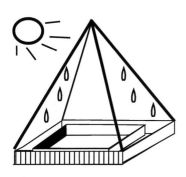

So sadly this advice will not benefit any of my readers outside of Mexico.

No no, I *dare* not tell you here how to distil 50° proof alcohol even more conveniently - using just a marrow, sugar, sultanas, a teacup and your kitchen freezer. So *please don't ask*....

Chapter 6

Creative YeoPod Collars

The flower pot is dead. Long live the YeoPod!

True, not everyone will have a florist on their doorstep who lusts to give away dozens of two and three gallon plastic tubs. Long ones, fat ones, thin ones... Entirely free.

> Though have you really, *truly* scoured the rich potential of the florists in your Yellow Pages?

So I will helpfully list your other opportunities, in a descending order of plausibility, and ascending order of improbability:

1. Compost or manure bags

Every time you buy a bag of compost, manure, peat (ouch!), topsoil or wood chip, you acquire a free bag.

Also... whenever you are afflicted with a large household gift at Christmas, it comes in a free tough plastic bag.

> Have you ever considered: The more we buy kitchen gadgets, the more we eat out? *But I digress...*

All can be crafted into collars, cut down, their bottoms slit and their sides stapled.

Do not be afraid to use transparent collars. They do not harm the plant. You'll simply be enchanted by a verdant mould, growing within the peripheral walls.

> As I may have said already...

2. Lino

You can get acres of old lino from a friendly carpet fitter or builder, free. They have to pay to discard it in a landfill site as trade waste.

(Or else, they must dump it in a beauty site and imperil their soul.)

Once, whale hide was widely used to grow tomatoes by Ring Culture methods. When whale lovers protested (or rather, whale hide became unavailable), it was replaced by lino, plastic and other synthetics.

Lino makes a superb collar.

It lasts almost forever. Of course, it's very tough. So you must carve it into a semi-circle, using a carpet knife or very sharp blade (see diagram). Do this only under parental supervision.

Drill holes in the sides (I use a cordless drill). Then lash each semi-circle into a cone with wire or nylon string.

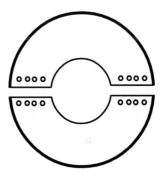

The good news is, you can take the cones up every season, stack them over Winter, scrub them with bleach... and use them again. And again.

3. Carpet offcuts

To cultivate a friendly carpet layer is an investment. Ply that good person with beer every week.

If you are in the UK, and VAT registered, this might be deemed a business transaction - *so can recover the VAT from your beer.*

He (and it still usually is a he) will then deliver to your door their every carpet offcut thereafter.

4. Plastic wastebins

Do *not* liberate these from hotel bedrooms. (You don't know what's been in them.) Instead, they can be had in job lots for mere pence at market stalls.

5. Tyres

Three small tyres, stacked, make an admirable - and indestructible - collar, if well washed.

Do not worry about toxins that may be present in the tyre material itself. Research suggests the toxin levels are insignificant and do not leach out much anyway.

Tyres also provide a great base for a typee or wigwam. Thrust a cane in the middle, tie strings to the top and splay them around the rim, like a little maypole.

Purists might wish to cut out the tyre walls with a sharp Stanley (packing case) knife. But I find this makes the tyre stack less robust.

A large tractor tyre will be entirely wasted as a YeoPod. Instead, corral your troublesome kiddies in it. (See Pests, Children. Chapter 18)

6. Cardboard or newspaper collars

Take a sheet of thick corrugated cardboard. Or a tabloid newspaper. Pull half the newspaper's pages halfway out, lengthways, so you have a long newspaper. Roll this into a collar and secure it temporarily with sellotape.

Do similarly if you use cardboard.

Plonk it atop a GrowCone and fill with potting mix. Then tie the collar more durably together with string or wire.

A thick collar of cardboard or newspaper will keep its shape for at least one season, and can then be torn into shreds and tossed on the compost heap.

If you tie it with degradeable jute string, the whole lot can be composted at season's end.

> **A tip:** to tear newspaper or cardboard into shreds easily, soak them - your spouse being absent - in a bathtub of water overnight.

7. Quality plastic bags

Kitchen waste bags and flimsy supermarket bags are - very wisely - designed to degrade in light.

> Though black plastic garbage bags last at least six months outdoors, I find.

However, the thick strong plastic shopping bags thrust upon you by quality shops will endure in the soil long enough to excite future archeologists.

> "Mr Harrod..." they'll tut in an alien tongue. *"Wasn't he the last Pharoah?"*

Cut off at the base, such bags make superb collars and are endlessly recyclable - at least, in your garden.

9. Big nylon mesh bags

If you buy bulk vegetables like potatoes in giant plastic mesh bags, congratulate yourself! Long after the vegetables have vanished from your taste buds, the bags can be doing duty in your garden.

Cut open, they will protect your brassica from caterpillars.

> *Or* truss up your melons.

> *Or* support your climbing beans and peas, if wired together on a trellis.

> *Or* let you pull up a tender perennial at season's end, to bring indoors over Winter - if you lay them under a collar.

Not least, they will make a collar.

It is not a very good collar, I admit. Dry potting mix will flop out of it and heavy rain will degrade its shape. But enough compost, if added when wet, will stay in place.

10. Washing up bowls, plastic storage boxes and other domestic detritus

A very good shallow collar for herbs, lettuces and other small plants may be made by cutting the base out of an otherwise derelict washing up bowl.

> *Or* deep refrigerator drawer.

> *Or* any plastic storage box that you might otherwise slide under the bed.

Not least, the rotary drum from a dead washing machine has exciting potential, and not just as a YeoPod collar. Imagine the sweet potatoes that might be grown therein, indoors, their lush vines twining around your window sills!

If your collar is *very* wide, of course, you will need to ram *two* adjacent GrowCones below it.

However, it is best - I whisper to you from pained experience - *to consult with one's spouse*, before hastily recycling kitchen artifacts into garden use.

11. Other excellent collars

Other excellent collars may be procured from roof tiles wired into square boxes or even old foam pillows, tied into fat collars with string. Their insulation properties should prove a boon to early transplants.

What's more, being absorbent, they

might even provide a supplementary water reservoir for lateral roots.

I feel a new book coming on: 'For the *Truly* Lazy Gardener - *Pillow* Bed Horticulture'.

Nor would I dissuade you from...

~ beer and cider kegs (cut in half and their bases removed),

~ plastic sewer pipes carved into sections,

~ hessian (burlap) sacks,

~ grandfather's top hat,

~ paper potato bags (very durable),

~ a child's plastic potty (a bog garden),

~ chimney pots,

~ woollen shirts (two small collars can be cut from each arm and the torso used for a jumbo-sized YeoPod),

~ wellie boots cut off at the ankle (each leg provides two slim collars, plus the perforated shoe portions can then be hung on a fence and tumbler tomatoes grown in them).

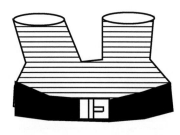

Moreover, it would be a sin to omit **denim jeans**.

A large pair of men's jeans will provide six small collars, if the legs are chopped, plus one very large collar with two skyward-facing orifices - if the seat portion is upended.

BiCameral Levis are capacious enough to grow two impressive tomato plants.

Levis will not usually degrade until Autumn and, being largely cotton, can then be thrown into the compost heap.

Trousers made from synthetics, of course, may prove even more durable... but be less satisfying to the soul.

Technically advanced collars

Very large plastic flower tubs with downturned rims can be turned into technically advanced collars. Remove the base and up-end them, then drill holes around the inner rim.

When it rains, water will collect in the rim and - instead of being wasted in the adjacent soil - will drain through the holes back into the YeoPod.

However, such tubs are very expensive (unless you beg a friendly garden centre to give you its damaged pots). They also violate the central principle of Yeomanry - joyful creativity *without* expense.

Neither will I explore here...

the potential for collars offered by roadside litter bins, Post Office mailbags or illuminated traffic bollards. They are **Someone Else's Property** and, besides... can more usefully be employed to grow potatoes in.

Chapter 7

The Aesthetic YeoPod

I was reluctant to share the following idea with you, lest you enter it at the Chelsea Flower Show and become famous.

From pained experience I can tell you that famous gardeners get **Repetitive Stress Injury** at book signings, then have to throw in the trowel.

I have only your interests at heart.

But if you insist, a very picturesque garden *can* be built using YeoPod collars - that are painted.

They can be colour coded lest you forget what you have planted there. Thus, red collars for tomatoes, green for cabbages, purple for broccoli, and the like.

If you wish your YeoPods to merge into the landscape, paint them in camouflage colours - green and brown. But if you seek a bold show of colour in any season - to match the purple decking on your patio - then red, yellow and orange are a must.

The nouveau riche gardener...

might flaunt silver, bronze or gold collars. Those who live in a yurt might prefer gentle earth tones - beige, weathered bone or adobe clay.

> A coating of cow manure and mud will also promote an almost instant display of algae, to give a pleasing 'aged' effect.

And what of textures, I ask?

Such as collars woven from straw? Or plaited with willow in

Celtic designs? Or inset with Hopi beads?

More work needs to be done in this important area.

Crop yield comparisons

More scientifically, you could also experiment with the productivity of plants grown in *different coloured* collars.

For example, black absorbs heat so might delight tomatoes and cucurbits.

White reflects heat so might - in a warm season - please cool-loving brassicas, lettuces and peas.

Red radiates beneficial light frequencies so might exalt the plants in adjacent YeoPods.

Yellow attracts whitefly and thrips so a yellow collar (or a white one is just as effective, research suggests) might be smeared with tanglefoot to trap pestilential insects.

You can make your own tanglefoot, it's said, by boiling molasses with linseed oil. Or better, by persuading somebody else to do it...

All beauty in a garden should conduce to utility. And as you see, a YeoPod is not only beautiful but *purposeful*..

Chapter 8

The Milk Bottle YeoPod

I have kept the Ultimate YeoPod till last.

It is just possible that some good folk - reading this on an ice floe - cannot procure any of the collars I have previously suggested.

> Do I hear you protest, YeoPods could not be made on an ice floe, either? *Psshaw*, lettuces have been known to germinate on slabs of ice. Alaskan Fancy tomatoes were bred precisely for such conditions!

But few gardeners in the world can fail to locate... a 2 litre plastic milk bottle.

> Or the equivalent - a 2-litre plastic cola, juice or cooking oil bottle.

A reader in Nepal once assured me they abound amid her most secluded mountains, even upon the top of Everest.

> Absolutely true. She built an acre of BottleBeds from them, she told me. (BottleBed technology is revealed in *The Lazy Kitchen Gardener*.)

Villagers throughout the world's most impoverished nations collect them to carry water. They wash up so frequently on the world's beaches - including ice floes - that oceanographers use them to chart sea currents.

They are totally weatherproof.

My vast collection...

stored outdoors, is now five years old and only the labels have perished. Such is their versatility in the home, workshop and garden that I have written a modest treatise upon them - *57 Practical Garden Uses for Old Plastic Milk Bottles* - that I will send to you on request, entirely free, when you join the Village Guild.

I concede, they are only half the volume of a florist's large 8 litre pail cut in half. So they will *not* grow you mighty squash, pumpkins or courgettes.

> Although who but a braggart would demand giant squash? Little ones are far more toothsome.

But they *will* rear as many tomatoes as you can eat, large leeks, respectable cabbages or sumptious heads of calabrese.

They also have fascinating built-in advantages, not possessed by other collars.

How to make a Milk Bottle YeoPod

Slice off the base of a 2-litre (or larger) empty plastic milk bottle. But leave one of the four sides uncut. Hinge this back as a flap.

Cut off the top of the bottle at the point where it starts to curve inwards towards the neck.

This gives you a collar with, moreover, a useful tube - open at top and bottom - where the handle had been. Cut the top rim of the bottle into crenellations, or sharp 'V' shapes, and bend them outwards. (This is Optional.)

Build a GrowCone in the usual way.

Ram a hole beside it for a cane. Put the collar over the cone, with the lower flap bent outwards, and push a cane through the handle part of the bottle.

> This is useful to secure it to the ground even if you *don't* grow climbing plants.

Fill the collar with the usual potting mix.

Now punch two holes in the protruding flap and push in a stiff wire staple eg. cut from a coathanger.

This is not essential and, in hard ground, it's difficult. But if your garden is subject to high winds, it gives further security against the collar twisting or toppling.

In that case, 'twould be wise to lay a brick on the flap as well.

What are the optional crenellations for?

First, they're pretty.

> Paint a face on the collar and, with its spikey hair, it will resemble a well-known cartoon character. This effect can be enhanced by growing trailing lobellia around the edge.

Second (and seriously), the little Vs deter snails and slugs. They really do.

Paint a band of grease mixed with salt or soot around the collar as well, and you should be totally mollusc-proof.

So prolifically available are plastic milk bottles that you could blanket your garden with them. Being rectangular, they can be abutted side by side - the better to suppress weeds.

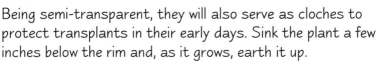

Being semi-transparent, they will also serve as cloches to protect transplants in their early days. Sink the plant a few inches below the rim and, as it grows, earth it up.

If you should conclude they have no further use as YeoPods (unlikely, I agree), take them up.

Wash them and slice the plastic into plant labels - or any other application that calls for small pieces of soft, strong, malleable, indestructible plastic sheeting.

Such as... washers for taps, dividers for seed modules or fastening strips for climbing tomatoes.

Not for nothing are plastic milk bottles honoured as one of the indispensable **Three Sisters of YeoPod Horticulture!**

The other two are, of course - as you will read abundantly in these pages - *nylon socks* and *pantihose*.

Chapter 9

The ultimate YeoTrellis - a YeoMattress

If you grow climbing plants, tradition has it that they demand artificial supports.

Pea twigs, canes, typees, trellises, children's swings, netting, even old Dad's bicycle will host a lusty legume. And legumes need support, don't they?

That is not necessarily true.

Grow dwarf peas in double (or, if you're greedy) triple rows, the rows four inches apart, and they will fall lovingly into each other's arms and need no other support. Of course.

Free lunch?

But grow *climbing* peas or beans in the same way, and they'll simply straggle over the ground and hang out a road sign 'Free lunch!' for every pestilential thing that creeps, festers or lurks.

> Yes, you'll get *some* crop - and that twining blob does make a great weed suppressant - but, for gardeners like us, there's no such thing as a free lunch.

Is there? Well, we can *still* negotiate a 'free lunch' - of a sort.

Simply sow your vining plants - legumes, squash, achocha (even nasturtiums, clematis, honeysuckle or sweet peas if you must) - in parallel rows of YeoPods, the rows around four, five or six feet apart.

> The width will be dictated by whatever bedstead you

might have to hand...

Bedstead?

At once, go to your council recycling tip and see what abandoned bedsteads lie there forlorn.

There is great poetry in a recycling tip.

Meditate humbly for a moment to consider... what awesome posterity those beds could, in their time, have fructified! What future Einsteins, Galileos, Pasteurs - indeed, what Yeomen - might have been conceived upon those rusty frames! You are about to accept a sacred charge.

Fortunately, the charge is quite small.

Pay the site attendant around £5 - at time of writing - and you can take the bedsteads home.

For a slightly larger sum, he might deliver them to your door. This is helpful, if you have acquired the frame of a king-sized bed.

Lay that frame...

above your rows of YeoPods so there is at least a six inch clearance between the collar top and the frame.

You may need to support the bed legs on bricks - or truss a strong wooden stave to each leg, to raise it even higher.

No matter. *Your labour is an Investment!*

As the plants grow, train them through the coiled wires and across the bed frame. Within two months, the frame will be a heaving mass of flowers and foliage. Its ugliness long gone, it will be unspeakably beautiful.

And underneath, will hang *glissades of pendulous fruit!*

Beans, peas, squash, melons, giant beefsteak tomatoes...

whatever you've sown. All protected therein from insect pests, weather and wild life.

Now comes the trcky part...

That thick canopy will also have suppressed most weeds.

Now comes the tricky part... *harvesting the crop.*

If your bedframe is a mere 15 inches above ground, you will need to dispatch beneath it a small child. Such helpers are unreliable.

'Twere better had you, at the outset, raised your bedframe at least three - or even four - foot above ground. And positioned your YeoPods at its periphery.

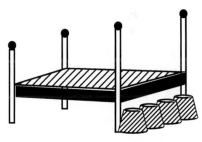

You can then inch upon your stomach within that jungle tunnel, a bag roped to your waist, turn upon your back - and pull your fruitful crop as it burgeons above you!

One of the most electrifying moments...

This can be one of the most electrifying moments in organic gardening.

You will now observe your garden from the perspective of the ant, the slug and the slow worm. You will feel At One with Nature. You will fall asleep, lulled by the murmur of bees.

Within your tropic paradise, no spouse can track you down. Nor bailiff find you.

That private retreat might give you much surcease from domestic strife, a whole season long.

Especially if you equip it with a portable television, fridge and laptop computer.

Truly, a YeoTrellis (kingsize) is a breakthrough in preserving marital felicity.

Seriously, it grows a lot of crops too - and a lot more easily than trussing canes into typees!

At season's end, simply toss the metal bedstead onto a bonfire. This will burn off the dead vines. It will also destroy any wooden supports.

Never mind. The metal frame will last *indefinitely*. Simply prop it up again, next Spring, upon new wooden staves.

The ash from burnt legume vines is also super-rich in potash, and could be bagged to use on squash next year.

If you insist on being conventional

Okay, if you insist upon being conventional you could, of course, make a trellis for YeoPods by inserting canes in or around the collars and affixing them in every manner of conventional trellis, cage or wigwam shape.

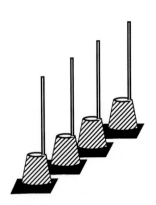

Or you might grow vining plants up sweet corn, sunflowers and jerusalem artichokes.

Provided the host plants are started several weeks earlier than the climbers, and all plants get lavish water, such companions do not harm each other, as we have seen.

But for a true student of Yeomanry, that's not original - nor is it fun.

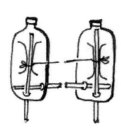

Just for fun, I include here a diagram of two ways to secure the tops of a cane trellis, using (left) plastic milk bottles or (right) cola cans.

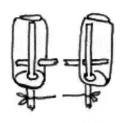

They will appeal especially to those folk whose trellis tops keep popping out of their securing string or wire. They are totally immune to the highest wind (if tied properly).

Alas, they are also very ugly.

To plant trailing lobelia in the base of the aerial pots is no remedy whatsoever, I find.

Chapter 10

How to propagate for YeoPods

Nature has been propagating seeds for millennia. All by itself.

Question: Why do we make it so difficult?

Answer: Nature has a few millennia more experience in this matter than we do.

One principle of the YeoPod is that it allows us to set out transplants into customised soil, and safely - removed from almost all the problems that a seed or rootball might face if it were planted in the open ground.

> A transplant is any plant you have propagated elsewhere, perhaps indoors or in a greenhouse, in some form of intermediary pot. And which you subsequently plonk outdoors.

That said, there's no reason *not* to sow seeds straight into a YeoPod collar. Provided you have mulched the top inch or so with sand or sterilised purchased compost, any large seed like a bean, pea, sunflower or squash will thrust its way through regardless.

It will flourish, unafflicted by weeds. And save you a lot of work.

> For many years, I insisted upon germinating my beans and peas indoors in modules. That is, little pots.
>
> Much labour and patience did it take. And it lead to much ensuing heartbreak when some 25% of the seed did *not* germinate - and their little empty cradles had to be recycled.
>
> It broke my heart.
>
> Nor could I accept the ethics of those who said, 'sow

three seeds per pot, then pinch out the two weaker plants'. Have they no soul?

I yearned to cherish those forlorn weaklings.

But one year I became tired of module growing. In a fit of pique, I broadcast-sowed a handful of bean seeds in a row, tossed soil on them - and I didn't come back for six weeks. So much for soul...

Of course, every darned one germinated.

Nor did rodents, birds or damping off disease afflict them. All grew lustily by themselves, without my dubious attentions.

Indeed, the Blauhilde bean seeds that I thrust recklessly into the soil, amidst rampant marestail fronds, did a *lot* better than those I'd carefully set out in modules in bare soil.

Did the marestail <u>shield</u> the young shoots from the sun?

A Guild member tells me she gets wondrous results, for that reason, growing strawberries - *within* lusty marestail. As the strawberries ripen, she simply breaks down the marestail and it becomes a bed, raising the fruit off the ground.

Could marestail really be a - much misunderstood - *gardener's friend?*

Since then, I have concluded - modules (or seed beds) *may* be essential for finicky or little seed. Or for rare seed, where you just can't afford to risk the vagaries of pests and the weather.

But usually, you *don't* need to grow your plants in several arduous stages as the textbooks advise... first in seedbeds, then thinning them out, then moving them to intermediate pots - before planting them out.

Nor do you (usually) need to harden them off!

> Does anyone *really* enjoy the labour of trotting their modules - grown indoors - in and out of doors for three weeks, at dawn and dusk, at increasingly extended intervals. To harden them off?

> Especially as, unless the weather proves fickle, 'hardening off' is almost always unnecessary.

Nature doesn't do any of that.

And it has done well enough, for millennia... by itself.

So, following Nature's way, *how can we best propagate our seeds for YeoPods?*

Seed trays will serve for plants that don't mind root disturbance, and indeed thrive on it - like brassica, leeks and lettuces.

Indeed, so robust is a young cabbage plant, you can tear it out of the seed tray, toss it on the soil, scoop a little soil over the roots.

Then dance all over it with football boots.

It will grow even the bushier, and love you the more, for your 'tough love'.

But other plants are best grown (more gently) in *little pots*.

Many triumphs have been achieved with yogurt pots, grapefruit shells (perforated), Rootrainers, foil-lined juice cartons, pockets cut from pantihose or nylon socks (stapled at the bottom), egg shell halves (cracked at the bottom), loo rolls (*half* rolls are best) and newspaper strips - wrapped around a bottle and taped or stapled into tubs.

I love them all.

Carrots and parsnips especially love newspaper, toilet rolls, and pots made from long nylon socks or nine-inch pockets of pantihose, all of which can be dropped straight into the soil.

> Do *shred* the nylon when planting it. And bury the degradeable pots *fully* - or the paper or card acts as a wick and dehydrates the plant.

Tubers - which dislike root disturbance - can also be germinated successfully in Rootrainers or slim foil-lined juice cartons (with a flap cut at one side to ease extraction of the rootball).

A simple and novel way to germinate almost any plant...

(of course), is in - a miniature YeoPod!

Take a small yogurt pot, turn it upside down, slice off the base. Put it on a board covered with a plastic sheet (this can be cut from an ordinary shopping bag). And fill with a pasteurised seedling mix.

When the plant has grown several true leaves (ie. not merely its seed leaves or *cotyledons*) and its roots just fill the pot, slide the pot off the board - holding the plastic sheet around it to retain the soil intact.

Bury it in a hole in the top of the soil-filled YeoPod collar but *without* removing the yogurt pot. And pull out the plastic sheet.

The pot remains in place as a mini inner collar.

The roots will then grow down into the outer collar and expand - but suffer almost no root disturbance.

This is far more efficient than growing in a perforated yogurt pot - or conventional flower pot - then trying to

shake the rootball out. Unless the plant is virtually
rootbound, half the pot contents will disintegrate around
one's feet, I find.

Any tubers can be grown by this method.

A YeoPod filled throughout with a friable mix, especially in
its GrowCone, might grow you a carrot 18 inches long, if
that's your aim.

For larger plants like tomatoes or squash...

use a 1 pint yogurt pot, or any other tall
plastic pot with its own lid - such as the
drinking cups discarded lavishly around
fast-food outlets.

Cut off the base as before *but keep the
lid in place* and perforate it. When time
comes to transplant, remove the lid and
plant the entire pot (now a collar).

Take that idea still further and you could *pre-plant* the final
YeoPod collar itself, indoors or in a greenhouse.

Set it in a board covered with a plastic sheet as before. Fill
it with a suitable potting mix. But this time make a cup-
sized hole in the mix at the top of
the collar.

Fill this 'cup' with a weak seedling
mix. Sow your seed directly into this
cup.

When the plant is some 4-6 inches
high and its roots are appearing at
the base of the collar, slide the collar
over the GrowCone outdoors, and
remove the plastic sheet.

The seed will then have ideal germination conditions, given appropriate light, warmth and humidity - which are easier to control under cover anyway.

It will first encounter weak soil then, as its roots develop into the collar, a stronger mix. It will finally gain its full nutrients as the roots sink into the GrowCone outdoors.

Incidentally, don't worry about collars, set upon a board, becoming waterlogged. There will be enough gaps around the lower rims to ensure good drainage.

To avoid the heartbreak of having to discard surplus seedlings, you could also *pre*-germinate the seed. In this way, *every* germinated seed you sow is likely to grow.

You will not have the wasted effort...

of filling and sowing pots where seed fails to 'take'. Or the embarrassment of sowing a seed tray where half the plants germinate at once and the rest do so leisurely only over subsequent weeks.

This problem of staggered germination is most prevalent among heirloom or home-saved seeds. They often have 'germination inhibitors' around their seed case.

These can be removed eg. with tomato and cucurbit seeds, by fermenting the seed. But it explains why old compost, tossed on the soil, invariably blooms with volunteers... last year's seed!

(At *last*, the seeds' germination inhibitors have rotted off.)

It's embarrassing because...

you might be germinating seeds in an 85°F airing cupboard. As soon as the first crook of a plant stem emerges, you rightly rush the tray into full light and cooler conditions to avoid the seedlings becoming leggy.

However, the other seeds would prefer to stay in the warmth and dark. So many won't germinate.

When the early-growing seedlings have grown lusty and must be removed from the tray, you can't help disturbing the just-emerging seedlings. So many of them die.

True, commercial growers succeed in growing many plants together in *one* segmented tray. But they use seed that's been selected to germinate simultaneously and they can control the germination conditions with a precision that's impossible for the amateur grower.

By *pre-germinating* your seed, you can ensure that virtually *any* seed that's ever going to germinate turns successfully into a plant. This is important if you sow rare seed, or your seed stock is small.

The simplest way to pre-germinate a small number of seeds...

is to take three saucers. Lay a twice-folded strip of damp kitchen paper in one saucer, and lead it into another saucer. Half  fill the second saucer with room-temperature water.

Drop a small amount of seed at equal intervals on the paper in the first saucer, keeping each seed apart.

Put an upturned saucer over that saucer, to exclude light and conserve humidity.

Leave this simple propagating device in a warm place. Around 75°F is ideal for most plants.

> Warm climate plants like tomatoes, peppers and cucurbits prefer 85°F. The ideal germination temperatures for most vegetables are given in Chapter 21.

Check it every day. Top up the water reservoir if necessary so the paper stays moist but does not drown the seed.

> That's why a *twice* folded strip is important. It has *four* thicknesses, which should stop the seed floating in water.

In as little as 2-3 days you may see the first sign of germination, a tiny root emerging. Pick the germinating seeds out carefully with a soft plastic 'spoon', such as a strip cut from a plastic milk bottle and crimped.

Drop each at once into its own pot or collar, made as above and filled with a damp seedling mix. A rule of thumb is, the seed should be buried at a depth *three times its width*.

> If you're not sure if that fragile emerging thing is a root or stem - plant it *sideways*.

Lay a sheet of absorbent card or newspaper over the pots and put them back in the same warm place. Check daily!

As soon as a shoot emerges...

rush that pot into a cooler place and full light.

> Leave it for just 24 hours longer and it may become hopelessly leggy.

Meanwhile, put the saucer back over those seeds that have *not* yet germinated and return the saucers to the warmth.

In this way, you can salvage almost *all* the seeds that are not dead or sterile. They'll happily grow on in their pots once germinated, provided nothing untoward happens.

> Of course, they can *still* be demotivated in their nursery by too much or too little watering, temperature extremes, or rough handling.

If you leave germinating seed too long in the saucer, its roots will get tangled in the paper. *Do not pull the roots out*. Cut out a little fragment of paper instead, and plant root, paper and seed together.

This is the simplest of all pre-germinating devices... apart from the **Perlite Pot**.

>   *What's that?* I hear you cry...

>   Simply fill a plastic margarine tub with damp perlite,
>   drop in the seed, seal the tub and toss it in the airing
>   cupboard for a few days, keeping a constant watch.
>   That works too, magnificently.

When enough shoots are showing, cast the lot onto a
sheet of newspaper and pick out each seedling carefully by
its leaves. Then dibber each into a deep hole in a pot, so the
leaves are just above the seedling mix.

Why must you wait till you see the shoots?

Because any germinated roots will be hidden in the perlite.

Problem is, you *do* waste a lot of seed that way.

It's very easy to germinate 1000 lettuce seedlings at once,
and to break your heart by throwing away the 980 you
don't need. Dibbering in a fragile seedling root is also very
laborious and demands the patience of an embroiderer.

However, to drop in a *seed* with just a small root showing is
faster, easier and safer.

The one drawback...

of the saucer method is that kitchen paper will rot after
about eight days. If much of your seed hasn't germinated
by then, you have to transfer it to a fresh sheet and start
again.

This inconvenience can be avoided if, instead of paper, you
use a 100% nylon sock or stocking. This never rots.

>   It just smells that way.

Truly, there is very little in the garden you *cannot* do... *with
an old nylon sock.*

Chapter 11

Companion planting for YeoPods

If only...

if only rational folk (like you and I) - who can make intelligent decisions about complex issues like pensions and the future of the planet - were equally rational about 'companion planting'!

We'd acknowledge that, yes, it *is* sometimes successful.

But its successes have little to do with mysterious secretions, vibrations, fragrances or cosmic influences... which might (or might not) mutually suppress or enhance the growth of a plant - grown adjacently.

We might reluctantly concede, its real benefits occur when plants of different families are grouped together into a **'guild'**.

> That's just a pretentious name for a clump of different, lonely, sad, mutually supporting plants growing together like freemasons

In a guild, each plant can enjoy the same type of soil or position in the garden, without interfering with each others' demands.

A guild is a Good Thing

Clumping plants of different families together in a guild, and in random patterns rather than rows, confuses pests. It suppresses them. It truly does.

So you might reasonably conclude, 'Companion planting works!'.

However, you could mix up *every* plant in the botanica at

random, and sow them together. Provided each plant liked much the same soil and climate, you'd probably get far fewer pest or disease problems than the same plants sown in separate blocks or rows.

So there's no need for rigid or quasi-scientific companion planting rules, is there? Especially as every 'rule', has been totally confuted - by somebody's experience, somewhere. For example:

Do tomatoes love brassica or hate them? Two different textbooks I have before me as I write give conflicting views.

Do alliums (onions, chives, garlic, etc) suppress beans? Most textbooks say they do. Yet a veteran market gardener, a Guild member (of the *Village* Guild, I hasten to add), tells me he has grown bush beans amongst onions for decades with no ill effect.

Do sunflowers have an allelopathic effect on adjacent plants (ie. they poison them)? One revered UK guru says they do.

So how come I've been growing climbing beans up sunflowers, and raising brassica at their roots - successfully, for several years?

Many of my members have done likewise, they tell me.

So after 30 years' experience, in every variety of garden, I have to conclude:

Companion planting is effective ONLY if...

~ the colours, shapes or fragrances of the companion plants deter or confuse flying insects. *Or...*

~ the root secretions of the companion plants repel burrowing insects.

No, planting caper spurge does *not* deter warm-blooded burrowing pests like moles. Just in case you asked...

Nor will I explore here the utility of encouraging nettles, thistles and brambles around your allotment patch to deter human pests. That should be termed *Un*Companionable Planting.

YeoPods are unsociable

YeoPods do not need much by way of companion plants, in the usual sense. Because they enjoy their own controlled environment. Immune to most pests.

I concede, there's no harm in twining nasturtiums up your bean poles, or sowing tall marigolds *(Calendula)* betwixt the YeoPods. As tradition dictates.

They'll add colour, and the leaves and flowers are deliciously edible. Of course, they won't deter a single insect pest. Worse, the nasturtiums will become a holiday home for caterpillars.

Fortunately, you can shake the caterpillars daily into your duck tractor. You *do* have a duck tractor, don't you?

The ONLY Companion Planting methods that reliably work

Only two companion methods are worth speaking of, in the same context as YeoPods. Because (like YeoPods) they work:

1. Mexican marigolds

Sow Mexican marigolds *(Tagetes minuta)* with moderation, in the tops of YeoPods, alongside other plants.

One or two will not harm the growth of the main plant in a large pod and their root secretions do - it has been proven - kill harmful nematodes and many burrowing insect pests.

They also kill couch grass, bindweed, ground elder and other perennial weeds (which you should not experience in a YeoPod anyway).

No other cultivar of Tagetes - or Calendula - reliably repels pests. It absolutely must be *Tagetes minuta.* Accept no substitutes.

2. Essential oils of companion plants

Why trouble to set out companion plants, which might mature fitfully (if at all) or at the wrong time to do any good, when you might distil and store - their **essences?**

Then spray them onto your plants - precisely when the plants are most vulnerable?

So for example...

to deter butterflies from cabbages, you might spray on them a distillate of any of the herbs usually recommended as brassica companion plants: caraway, celery, chamomile, coriander, dill, hyssop, marjoram, rosemary, Summer savory or thyme.

You will note, these are all smelly substances. So the question arises, will *any* confusing odour also... repel butterflies?

Probably, yes.

To make an essence of any herb...

soak it in sunflower oil - or any other mild vegetable oil - in warmth for a few weeks.

> I have also read that supermarket vodka (otherwise useless, except for cleaning computer keyboards) can perform the same trick.

Then strain it through muslin - or the sleeve of an old cotton shirt - and store the oil in a sealed jar in a fridge.

For use, it can be diluted in further oil or water, respectively. But anyone with serious bugs will just rush to zap them with that distillate straight from the bottle, I suspect...

A tip: Spray any oil-based distillate on your plants

through one of those pump-action kitchen gadgets that are sold to lazy chefs for spraying vinaigrette onto salads.

My water spray gun clogged at once, using oil.

If instead you spray a *water*-based infusion, wire a little pod of muslin around the base of the inlet tube in your spray gun. Or it too will - I find - soon clog with muck.

Those are the only two recommendations about Companion Planting that have, in the documented History of Mankind, ever made any consistent sense whatsoever.

They are the *only* ones you can rely on. I give you my word on that.

By the way, the advice in this Chapter will work *anywhere* in your garden - even if (inexplicably) you *don't* use YeoPods!

Chapter 12

Crop rotation in a YeoPod

What do you do with your YeoPods at end of the season?

There's no doubt that a gardenful of naked pots, shorn of their camouflaging weeds, can look a little stark. Nay, *ugly*.

Had you painted them in pleasing colours, of course, that might have been less of a problem. You would now have a **Structuralist Garden**!

> A Structuralist Garden is what local councils do when sowing ornamental cabbages in concrete raised beds. They believe it will engender Community Spirit.

Gardens are *supposed* to look ugly in Winter, however.

That way, we all enjoy better the advent of Spring. Purists could always take up the collars in Autumn, sieve out and compost the roots, and bag up the contents to use as topsoil next year.

An entirely new batch of YeoPods can then be started in Spring. If they're rammed into new ground, the GrowCones with their fresh nutrients will - year after year - refresh the ground.

The old collar mix will have few nutrients left but can usefully add texture to a weak seedling mix, if pasteurised. The collars and canes can be sterilised with a quick scrub and a soak in diluted bleach (chlorine) or Jeyes solution (formaldehyde).

Sterilisation?

You may be one of the many lucky gardeners who will *never* have disease transmitted by infected pots. Sterilisation, I concede, may be unnecessary if your plants were previously unafflicted by disease.

But if there was the slightest hint of disease last year, especially blight... sterilise! *(Do it anyway.)*

The sterilised collars can then be stacked out of sight over Winter, behind Dad's bicycle in the garage.

Failing that (and disease permitting), you can keep the collars where they are and grow in them again, for at least one further season - by adapting the principles of conventional crop rotation.

A *wise counsel*

Whoever first propounded the familiar three or four-year Crop Rotation was very wise.

(It might have been Yeo-tze...)

It was devised to minimise the problems of *diseases* and *pests* accumulating in the soil, which might occur if host crops of the same family were planted in the same beds year after year.

Another benefit of rotation is that plants of dissimilar families tend to take different *nutrients* from the soil, and require different soil amendments.

For example, it's often advised to start a new bed by digging in massive amounts of rotted manure or compost as early as possible, ideally in Autumn.

In our first growing year (let's call it **year A)**, we grow heavy feeders like potatoes, squash, outdoor melons, sweetcorn, tomatoes, comfrey and the like.

They don't mind a slightly acidic soil and can - arguably - devour, at their roots, even raw kitchen waste and sewage.

In **Year B**, we plant alliums (onions, shallots, leeks, garlic) and legumes (beans and peas). They like rich well drained soil, but are moderate feeders. They can subsist well enough on the aged rot - and soil nutrients - left behind by the prior crops.

They *don't* like acid soil, however, so lime or wood ash is often recommended to counter any acidity left by the aged rot...

In **Year C**, we grow heavy nitrogen-feeders - swedes, turnips, cabbages, broccoli, brussel sprouts, cauliflower and other brassica with fleshy leaves. In theory, they *should* benefit from the nitrogenous nodules left in the soil by the legumes. (But this is Received Wisdom, *so trust it not.*)

In **Year D**, we plant light feeders that much dislike lime, manure (and even aged rot) - carrots, parsnips, beetroot, lettuce, spinach and swiss chard.

In the fifth year, we start again.

In principle, we should not need to refresh the soil again in any way - apart from a little lime in year two - for four years.

Rotation is imperfect

In practice, of course, extracting the plants - their leaves, pods or fruits - will take from the soil so many nutrients - nitrogen, phosphorous and potassium (potash) in particular - that we must put back at least some of those nutrients every year.

Carpeting the soil with an inch of compost or other organic matter every Autumn is one of the easiest ways.

Alas, that's impractical with YeoPods.

Nor can we grow plants in the *same* YeoPod for four years

without refreshing the soil, even with meticulous rotation.

But we *can* grow plants successfully in the same GrowCones at least over two years - by replacing the contents of the collars.

If we're careful with our rotation.

Once we've pulled out the roots of the previous plant, we're left with a mostly empty collar plus a GrowCone that's half full of fibrous material and old potting mix. The contents should now be reasonably friable with much improved drainage, especially if worms have been at work.

Our soil is already improved!

Yes, replenish the GrowCone with whatever mix is apt to the intended new plant. But **No**, do *not* plant there next year anything of the same family - or in the same rotation - as you have just grown.

This is not so much a matter of making best use of the remaining nutrients. Most of them will be replaced with new mix anyway.

It's a question of pests and disease.

For example...

Had you grown potatoes in one GrowCone, perhaps using a pagoda of collars, you would not replace them with tomatoes or peppers. Potatoes, tomatoes and peppers are of the same *Solanaceae* family and share the same pests and diseases.

> For example, from pained experience I tell you, just one tiny blighted potato left in the soil will infect your next season's tomatoes with blight. *I guarantee it.*

Had you grown cabbages you would not move on to turnips,

kohlrabi or swedes (rutabaga). Black rot, clubroot and downy mildew are just a few of the many ailments they have in common and will (they *will*, I promise you) pass on to the next generation.

Because all are brassica.

A Safer Rotation

However, had you grown peas or beans in your YeoPods you might safely follow them with carrots or parsnips. They do not have many pests or diseases in common with legumes.

Moreover, they'll enjoy what residual nitrogenous nodules might have been left by the legumes.

Had you reared potatoes therein, you should have little trouble in growing there - next season - swedes, turnips, kohl rabi, cabbages, broccoli, kale or brussel sprouts.

Had you raised tomatoes, you could safely plant into their holes next season... broad beans, or indeed *any* beans or peas.

True, tomatoes are one of the few plants that *love* growing in their own waste. They adore compost made from their own rotted leaves. 'Tis said.

So in theory you could replant tomatoes in the same hole, year after year. But that assumes, the soil has never suffered any tomato pests or diseases.

Alas, in the real world, your garden and mine, *that rarely happens...*

Moral: you can indeed rotate plants within YeoPods - without taking them up or totally replenishing the soil - year after year. Just be *canny* about it!

For full details of what you might plant to precede - or succeed - any vegetable grown in YeoPods, see Chapter 21.

Chapter 13

The YeoPod SoilMix Recipe Book

Are you really, *truly* sure your soil is terrible?

Perhaps it just has a bad character, but it hides a heart of gold.

This book starts with the worst case assumption that your soil is a total rogue. Yet, I concede, I may be wrong. Your soil may be an angel. Despite its ugly appearance (and grim performance to date), it could be in excellent shape.

Fertile, friable and just waiting to be loved. In that case:

> *For you...* YeoPods will ease the chores of digging, watering and weeding.

> *For the plants...* YeoPods will concentrate water and nutrients exactly where the plants need them, at the roots. And the YeoPod design has resistance to many pests and predators 'built in'.

> *For the soil...* YeoPods will improve its texture, drainage and fertility - year after year. The more YeoPods you make, their contents retained to enrich the soil, the happier your soil will be.

One day, if your soil has been continuously improved by YeoPods, you may indeed be able to return to 'normal' gardening - in open soil. Even if you started with the worst possible soil.

Little fortresses

As you've read, YeoPods are little fortresses with their own micro-climates, which you can enhance still further (if you wish) with cloches, fleeces or nets.

So even if you have 'perfect' soil but weed or pest problems (and the more fertile your soil is, the more you'll have them) YeoPods will still improve your results, reduce your labour - and ease your back.

Needless to say, few of us have perfect soil.

I've heard folk say "my land is so fertile, weed and pest free that I just scatter seed in Spring, take a six month holiday and don't ever do anything else - except harvest the crop in Autumn".

The fisherman's tale

This is usually a gardener's variation on the fisherman's tale. ("You should have seen the cabbage that got away...")

But they're not necessarily lying.

Deep mulch methods *can* achieve that, in time. But folk usually go on to confess "it took three generations of my family 50 years - to get it to that condition".

More likely, folk will mourn "my soil's so bad that, if I set out a rock garden, *even the rocks die*".

How bad is your soil?

Try this painless experiment, ideally in Spring or Summer, especially if you've just acquired land you're unfamiliar with:

1. Is my soil fertile?

A few days after heavy rain, inspect the soil.

Is every square inch covered with a large variety of tall lusty weeds? That's fertile soil. *Rejoice!*

You can also be sure of its fertility if your weeds are predominantly fat hen (pigweed or lamb's quarters), dead nettles, purslane, burdock, dandelion, chicory, chickweed, Queen Anne's lace (wild carrot) or ragweed.

But your soil probably has *low* fertility if it's blistered with patches of bare earth and the few weeds visible are fennel, sorrel, chamomile, groundsel or plantain.

A laborious way...

to check your soil fertility is (if you are a man) to persuade a strong woman to dig a hole exactly one foot square and deep, when the soil is moist - then sift that soil through a fine sieve and count the number of earthworms present.

Men don't have the patience for this.

You might ingenuously suggest this to a high school teacher as a class project. If the boys put on a macho performance with their spades, while the girls count the worms (or, more plausibly, *vice versa*)... your garden will soon be dug for you.

Am I not wicked?

A dozen or more worms is an excellent sign of fertility. Few or no worms mean little soil food is present, for either worms or plants. That's Poor Soil.

An easier if less scientific approach is...

to ram a garden fork in the soil and bang the handle gently several times with a mallet. Thinking it's raining, randy worms will come to the surface to breed.

If after several minutes of this you see no worms, either you haven't got many worms anyway - or they have a headache.

2. What soil pH do I have?

The soil acidity or alkalinity of a soil (the pH) is not too important when you grow in YeoPods. Because YeoPods create their *own* micro-environment.

But it *is* important to know... if the adjacent soil is *toxically* high or low in pH.

Because the roots of plants grown in YeoPods will, at some point, venture into that adjacent soil.

If they meet a horribly acid soil of, say, pH 4 or below (*ouch!*) or (far more rarely) a grossly alkaline soil of pH 8.5 or above, the plant will not do well. YeoPod or not.

Please relax. *It won't happen.*

Virtually *no* soils are that bad, unless you're trying to garden over a toxic waste tip. In that case, call your local council at once. You are sitting on a notifiable health hazard!

But it is still nice, to know... what *kind* of soil you have bought, rented or inherited.

You can observe a lot, by looking

Before you rush to do a soil analysis (see below), you can observe a lot about your soil's relative acidity or alkalinity (pH) - *just by looking.*

Acid soil (pH well below 7)...

might be festooned with dock *(Rumex crispus)*, marestail *(Equisetum arvens)*, hawkweed *(Hieracium aurantiacum)*, ox-eye daisy *(Chrysanthemum leucanthemum)*, sow thistle *(Sonchus v.)*, knotweed *(Polygonum persicaria)*, plantain *(Plantago major)*, sorrel *(Rumex acetosella)* or groundsel *(Senecio vulgaris)*.

Alkaline soil (pH above 7)...

may be carpeted with goosefoot *(Chenopodium v.)*, fat hen *(Chenopodium album)*, chamomile *(Anthemis nobilis)*, bladder campion *(Silene latifolia)*, salad burnet *(Pimpinella saxifraga)* or coltsfoot *(Tussilago farfara)*.

There's nothing wrong with a soil being acid or alkaline (at least, within a pH range of around 5.5 - 8), if that's its only major problem.

An *acid* but fertile soil that's growing a forest of dock and sow thistle may yield you wondrous potatoes or strawberries.

An *alkaline* soil that's adorned with fat hen may also produce king-sized asparagus and leeks. What's more, you can cook all three together into a novel vichyssoise!

And delicious it is, too... though Escoffier would never acknowledge it.

A crude but interesting way

A crude but interesting way to test your soil pH is with beetroot juice. Put some slices of fresh beetroot in a glass with boiled or filtered water, or rain water (the lime present in tap water will skew the results). Let soak for ten minutes.

Mix a teaspoonful of soil with 10ml of similar water. Let it settle. Drop in some of the beetroot water.

If the colour turns more blue, you have alkaline soil. If it becomes redder, your soil is acid. If there's no colour change, your soil is neutral.

This test should also work using red cabbage but, as my family disdains it, I have never had occasion to grow it. So I can't say.

Of course, the **Beetroot Test** is not as accurate as a purchased pH testing kit (which is still not very accurate) or, better, a pH meter having two metal probes (ditto).

Results from even these devices, I find, can be ambiguous. Your soil pH may seem to oscillate from 5 to 7 between two samples... just a yard apart.

So if you *must* know precisely the composition of your soil,
there's no alternative but to invest in a professional
analysis from one of the firms that advertise in gardening
magazines. And follow their instructions for taking the soil
sample.

So frightening will their analysis be...

revealing that your soil is worse than battery acid and
shamefully deficient in every trace mineral from boron to
zircon - that you will at once become a lifelong advocate of
YeoPods.

No, you will *not* need to rotavate tons of lime, sulphur,
Growmore, manure, compost or calcified seaweed into your
soil every year for the next several aeons, to amend the soil
pH, N-P-K ratio and trace nutrients. As the firm might
suggest.

Because (you will gratefully recall)... deficiencies in the
adjacent soil, within reason, *don't trouble a YeoPod!*

3. How water retentive is my soil?

This is worth checking, because a soil that's pure clay or silt
will not drain well. If you use YeoPods, water may
accumulate in the GrowCone.

Luckily, this is an advantage.

The roots will then have a continual reservoir to sustain
them and you will need to water less often - or conceivably
not at all.

However, soil that's high in sand may drain *too* quickly. The
balanced mix in the GrowCone will retain water for a while,
but you will need to be more attentive to signs of water
shortage in hot weather - like wilting leaves.

Leaves are *supposed* to wilt on very hot days.

It's Nature's way of conserving water. But they should be robust again next day in the cool hours of dawn. If they *still* wilt, when the lark first sings, they urgently need water.

A *fast way to check on soil moisture...*

is to plunge your forefinger into the soil at least three inches deep ie. right up to your hand. If your fingertip comes out moist and stained, the soil has enough water to sustain the plants. For a while, at least.

But if the soil flakes off your fingertip and leaves little stain, it needs watering. At once.

We shall return to this exciting topic in another Chapter.

The classic way to check the soil composition is to put a large handful of soil in a tall slim glass jar with a lid. Fill with water, replace lid and shake.

Wait for at least an hour till all has settled.

At the bottom, you will see a layer of stones, above that coarse sand and above that layer fine sand. Atop that will be a darkish brown layer of clay or silt. (Silt is sedimentary clay that has been deposited by rivers).

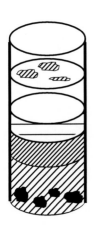

Then the water should be clear, with organic muck of various kinds floating on the surface.

If the sand layers are deeper than the clay layers, your soil is sandy. It may drain away too quickly.

If the reverse, it is a clay soil and you may face drainage problems.

If both layers are equal, your soil is well balanced. It should drain well but slowly.

A lot of floating organic muck means a lot of humus (decayed matter). This means your soil - all else being equal - should be very fertile. If not this year, then next year...

If a little duck floats on the surface, you have **Children**. See *Pests* (Chapter 18).

However... to mean anything at all, this test should be applied to soil samples taken at different parts of your garden and at various depths.

As you will recall, much of my 'problem' soil is a delightful balanced loam rich in clay, sand and humus - down to one inch. Then it turns by *degrees* into solid clay and flint. Eight inches deeper it is little more than chalk.

A soil sample taken from my top inch alone would be very misleading.

Another classic test is...

to mix a handful of soil with water till it has the consistency of putty.

Squeeze it into a ball.

If it refuses to hold its shape, that's a sandy soil.

If the ball crumbles apart very slowly as it dries, that's a balanced soil.

If it holds its shape even when dry and feels somewhat sticky when moist, it is a clay soil.

If you can roll it into a sausage, that also retains its shape as it dries, that's a very clay soil.

If you can squeeze that sausage into a bootlace and plait it into a Meissen vase, *abandon your garden*. Open a china clay factory instead...

The simplest test

The simplest test is just to ram in a GrowCone, fill it with water, and watch how fast it drains.

If the water vanishes at once, that's sand.

If it's gone in five minutes, that's a healthy balanced texture. But...

if the cone is still half full 30 minutes later, either you have a high water table, or stubborn clay - *or your soil is upside down*. It's *all* hardpan.

Never mind. A YeoPod will still cope...

What mixtures should go in a YeoPod?

That is the quintessential question.

Our aim is to create the ideal protected growing environment for every plant, regardless of how hostile or unpromising the adjacent soil may be.

Collars of various sizes enable us to expand that environment to accommodate almost any plant. But our results will depend almost entirely on the composition of the soil mix *in* the YeoPod.

Fortunately, we can control it to a *degree* that's impossible to match in the open soil - at least, without vast labour - and which approaches the precision of a hydroponic laboratory.

Better, our soil-based plants will enjoy trace nutrients and beneficial microorganisms unknown to plants grown in hydroponic chemicals.

We can choose to be as technical or simplistic - or as adventurous or lazy - as we wish.

The final book on YeoPod formulations will, I'm sure, be as

vast as the *Larousse Gastronomique* (and prove even more enlightening for those who can't read French).

Some basic recipes

Forgive me, therefore, if I suggest here merely some basic YeoPod recipes to whet your appetite for further - fascinating - experiment.

1. An Emergency Mix

If you have nothing else to hand. *And...* you have won a dozen over-leggy tomato plants at your local fête late in the season, and they must Go Out Now, there's nothing for it but...

to buy some bags of commercial compost.

This compost will work after a fashion, by itself, but it is sterile. All soil bacteria has been cooked out of it.

> Incidentally, if you *must* sterilise some topsoil or potting mix - perhaps to use in seed trays or as a weed-suppressing top mulch for containers - do *not* bake it for 20 minutes at high heat in the oven.
>
> As I once foolishly advised...

> To be organically kosher, *pasteurise it with steam.*

> Place it in a large metal kitchen colander, lined with pantihose, and held over boiling water for 20 minutes in a saucepan with its lid on. Periodically mix that gooey mass with a spoon and, for safety's sake, do wear kitchen gloves.

> A steam temperature of 99°C kills weed seeds and insect pests but leaves most of the beneficial bacteria alive.

> The process must be repeated several times to yield a useful quantity, scalds your wrists and makes your

kitchen stink. So it is best done outdoors over an open fire, *by somebody else.*

At this point, you might reasonably ask "do I really want to preserve my beneficial soil bacteria, *that badly?*")

2. An enhanced Emergency Mix - JY3

Any purchased compost can be enriched by mixing in top soil and aged cow manure, in the respective proportions 2:1:1.

The manure adds phosphorous plus useful soil bacteria, usually absent from purchased compost.

If you don't have cow manure, *any* farmyard, rabbit or guinea pig manure will do - but go easy on the poultry or pigeon droppings.

> Bird manure is the most nitrogenous of all farmyard manures. It can make young plants grow as exuberant as a new Cabinet Minister. But similarly, they yield no fruit - *then topple over.*
>
> For example, if you grow legumes, you'll get lusty leaves but few pods. Tomatoes grown in pigeon manure might enwrap your house, but they'll go down faster with fungal diseases. And they'll bequeath you nary a fruit.
>
> I speak from horrid experience...

The above is quite a rich mix.

Heavy feeders will love it - folk like tomatoes, squash, cucurbits and the like. Let's call this mix **JY3** - after the style of John Innes No 3.

A lighter mix using purchased compost - JY2.

If you don't have access to manure, here's a lighter mix.

Purchased compost mixed with sieved top soil and sand (or

perlite or vermiculite) in proportions 2:1:1 will suffice, for most plants.

This light mix will please most vegetables, especially if they get a little liquid feeding later. (See Chapter 16.) Let's call this mix **JY2.**

Even if your topsoil is relatively infertile, that topsoil can *still* be used in a YeoPod mix - in the proportions above. (Provided it's not actively toxic, of course.) It then becomes a buffer ingredient, adding its own little dollops of soil minerals and bacteria, if little else.

In that case, you'll just have to step up the liquid feeding later

I stress, these two quick-fix options are for Emergencies only.

There are far better solutions.

After all, one of the many delightful principles of YeoPod gardening is... it enables us to create a perfect micro-environment for our plants. *Without* labour!

So let's explore some other options.

3. A basic mix - JY3A.

A Victorian formula suggests we mix together equal parts of well rotted manure, home made compost plus leaf mould - or crumbs from inside an old tree or stump. Then add a small quantity of sand, for drainage.

There is nothing wrong with this mix.

But it is very rich and best used for heavy feeders. Let's call it **JY3A** (*and why not, I ask?*).

> **Please note:** Any mix that uses a lot of woody material or fresh leaf mould - which continue to rot down - should also have a *lot* of nitrogenous material in it, like manure, to help it rot. *This mix does.*

4. A light mix for seedlings - JY1

Another but much lighter formula suggested by Mel Bartholomew in *Square Foot Gardening* is:

> 1 pailful *each* of... peat, sand, leaf mould, topsoil, vermiculite (or perlite)
> 2 cups fertiliser
> 1 cup lime (if the ground is acidic, its pH being below 6.5)
> ½ part woodash or charcoal.
>
> 'Fertiliser' in Mel's admirable book means formulations of varying strengths, but *all* comprising blood meal, bone meal, wood ashes and leaf mould.

Peat is controversial, of course. It's acidic, contains few nutrients, repels water when dry and is too powdery to improve drainage. It's also a largely irreplaceable resource and its extraction harms the environment.

One alternative is coir.

It's less acidic, absorbs water, helps drainage and is a renewable resource.

Leaf mould is another peat substitute but is quite acidic, especially if taken from conifers. So, unless your topsoil is very alkaline, it should always be mixed with lime, powdered egg shells or wood ash.

> Personally, I've found that dried and powdered sunflower heads - or corn cobs - do the same job as peat, equally well. But for that, you need to grow a lot of sunflowers... or sweet corn.
>
> Dried moss scraped off your roof works too. But to get enough of it, you need to be a roofer. Or own a *lot* of houses.

As Mel makes clear, this formula is fine for young or seedling plants - but any mature heavy feeder like a squash or beefsteak tomato would grow famished on it. And, like

Oliver, soon demand *more...*

So let's call this very light seedling mix **JY1**.

4. A Rough & Ready Mix - JY4

For the gardener who doesn't like fuss, this simple formula will work well enough for almost any vegetable:

2 gallons sieved topsoil
2 gallons aged, crumbled leaf mould
2 gallons home-made compost or aged manure
1 cup bonemeal
2 cups seaweed meal
½ cup calcified seaweed, ground limestone or dolomite (but only if the soil is acidic)

> Did you know that calcified seaweed is *not* seaweed at all, but a form of coral?

I have this from the excellent book *The Simple Guide to Organic Gardening*, Bob Sherman, Collins & Brown. Let's call this mix, for no particular reason, **JY4**.

It makes a simpler alternative to **JY5** (below) but, for clever folk like you and I, it is less intellectually challenging.

5. A Scientific Mix

Few of us have access to exotic ingredients like dried shrimp heads, silkworm cocoons, dried jellyfish, olive pomace, starfish or sardine scrap.

Though all are super-rich in various nutrients and I can divulge to you the N-P-K ratios for each, if you absolutely insist. (See Chapter 17.)

For us simple (albeit clever) folk, it is far more valuable to know that the richest organic sources of potash (potassium) are, in descending order of richness, the ash from...

> ~ burnt banana skins (and stems) - around 50%;
> ~ bracken, corncobs, cucumber skins, citrus and potato peel - around 30%;
> ~ bean and pea vines and pods - around 18%.

If we have a glut of such materials at season's end - and we plan to grow potash-lovers like squash, cucumbers, tomatoes and the like next year - it might truly make more sense to toss those ingredients into a *garden incinerator* than the compost heap.

We could then save the thoroughly dry ash in a sealed can or plastic bag (moist ash degrades quickly) to enrich our YeoPod mixes with next year.

Victorian gardeners swore by 'burnt soil' as a fabulous fertiliser. Provided that soil had been rich in organic matter, especially manure, *it was true.*

> Of course, the arguable practice of burning good soil and releasing so many of its nutrients into the air can *only* be justified in an emergency - if other nutrients are not to hand, and if fertility has to be shifted around the garden quickly.

Your 'all-purpose' YeoPod mix - JY5.

At last! JY5 is the formula you've been waiting for:

It will serve most vegetables magnificently. We can then readily improve it in small ways, to meet any special needs of certain vegetables, if we wish.

The 'all-purpose' YeoPod mix relies upon organic ingredients easily accessible to most people, whether in towns or the country.

> I have also suggested alternatives in most cases.

Above all, it does *not* demand topsoil which - in many gardens - may not be available.

I freely acknowledge Mel Bartholomew as my original
inspiration for this mix. However, I have adjusted it - from
experience - in many creative ways to suit the needs of a
YeoPod.

Does it work?

This is more or less the mix I used one year to grow *220*
heirloom tomatoes in YeoPods, plus sundry other
vegetables .

> And in subsequent years to grow out no fewer than *110 different*
> varieties of rare heirloom legumes, year on year. *Magnificently!*

Of course, I amended the mixes - creatively. You will hear of
these refinements as I proceed.

The 'all-purpose' YeoMix (based on Mel's mix) comprises:

> 10 parts of coir
> 6 parts of vermiculite or perlite.
> 4 parts of sand.
> 1 part of wood ash and/or charcoal.
> 8 parts of home-made compost.
> 1/20th part of lime.
> 1/20th part of organic fertiliser.

And here are my creative alternatives to the above mix..

10 parts of coir (Mel's mix).

My better alternatives are... nettles, comfrey, or other
mildly fibrous weeds. *Or* the stems and foliage of legumes.
Or moss scraped from your roof or pond sides. *Or* leaf
mould.

All dried and crudely chopped. (See **Note**, at end of
Chapter.)

> Most are far more nutritious in the soil than coir, improve porosity,
> work just as well - and, unlike coir, cost you nothing.

6 parts of vermiculite or perlite.

That can be expensive, unless you buy it in bulk from a horticultural wholesaler.

So my proposed substitutes are... dried sunflower heads, or jerusalem artichoke or hollyhock stems, or corn cobs, chopped into one-inch chunks and whirled briefly through a powerful kitchen blender.

> Do note... I mean *powerful.* Tough vegetable fibres will burn out a cheap blender. *This can distress your spouse....*

The crumbs absorb water and improve porosity.

Although they *do* rot down, and rob a little nitrogen from the mix, the lost nitrogen will be compensated for by other ingredients.

Coarse grit is another substitute for vermiculite or perlite.

Pssst... let it be whispered...

Even polyfoam packaging can be carved into chunks and buzzed into crumbs in the kitchen blender to yield a sterile drainage improver.

> Do dampen it first, or you'll be hoovering polystyrene dust out of your curtains forever.

That idea will horrify organic growers.

I agree, polystyrene crumbs are not absorbent. They do nothing for the soil. They are ethically repugnant to many folk, being derived from oil - a non-renewable resource.

But, darn it, *they don't harm the soil either.* Exactly the same can be said for so-called 'organic' drainage improvers - like stones, sand and grit. *Can't it?*

4 parts of sand.

'Sharp' builder's sand is best - the gross kind with little lumps plus flecks of mica in it. Very fine sand is Not Good. It tends to compact - and turn clay into pottery.

1 part of wood ash and/or charcoal.

The residue from a garden bonfire will suffice, provided only paper, wood or garden refuse was burned (ie. nothing plastic, rubber or chemical).

Sieve it very well to remove any large chunks of charcoal. These can be bagged for the fireplace - or next year's barbecue.

Even ash from your grate will do - provided it contains no more than 25% coal ash.

> Coal contains sulphur, bitumen and other undesirable ingredients.

Wood ash adds a lot of potash (potassium).

The charcoal, like wood ash, also reduces any acidity that might develop if you've used leaf mould. *Or* if your GrowCone has been rammed into super-hard clay and becomes water logged.

If you *don't* have wood ash or charcoal... lime or powdered egg shells (see below) will serve well enough for most purposes.

8 parts of home-made compost.

Sift this as well. But there's absolutely no need to use a fine sieve.

> I use a coarse half-inch mesh, taken from the door of my little daughter's guinea pig run. I place it over a wheelbarrow and it works fine. Meanwhile, the liberated guinea pigs have a ball... *and some even come back!*

Any totally gross thing, and matter that has not decomposed, can be tossed back into the compost heap.

> **Have you noticed?** Even the finest home-made compost contains chunks of wood. Always. Yet you *know* it was made solely from genteel kitchen waste, cardboard and lawn clippings.

> *So where did the wood come from?* Does compost, compressed by heat

and pressure, *create* wood? To this enduring conundrum, propounded over millennia, answer comes there none. *(Sorry I digress...)*

1/20th part of lime.

You won't need this, if you've already used wood ash (see above). But if you haven't, it's a wise option unless your adjacent soil is very alkaline.

If you have no lime, substitute powdered egg shells. The eggs can come from any race of poultry, including ostriches.

To powder egg shells:

Every time you crack an egg, drop the shells - unwashed - into a dish. Bake them in a microwave at full power for four minutes. Store them in a sealed jar.

When you have a full jar, drop them in the kitchen blender and whizz until they are powder. They are virtually pure lime - and can be used anywhere that garden lime is indicated.

A note for my readers in Florida: this does *not* work with alligator eggs.

1/20th part of organic fertiliser.

Well, I cite this only because Mel's book does.

But I found it wholly unnecessary to add his 'fertiliser' mixes of blood meal (nitrogen) and bone meal (phosphorous), wood ashes (potassium), and leaf mould.

Why? Because if you have good home-made compost, much of those nutrients should already be present!

Only if you're *unsure* of your compost would I recommend that you add an equal quantity of bone and blood meal - to comprise together one 1/20th part.

Do wear gloves when handling bone or blood meal. It's *supposed* to be sterilised, but...

Confused?

Okay, here again is the basic YeoPod mix (in its virgin state, before my creative amendments):

10 parts of coir.
6 parts of vermiculite or perlite.
4 parts of sand.
1 part of wood ash and/or charcoal.
8 parts of home-made compost.
1/20th part of lime.
1/20th part of organic fertiliser - principally bone meal mixed with blood meal.

But... to save your labour and expense, *do* substitute for these ingredients those I have suggested above...

The observant reader will note... that topsoil is *not* included in my suggestions above.

That's because I assume your topsoil is horrible or you have none. If you *do* have good friable loam (topsoil containing rich organic matter), of course, mix it in proportions 1:2 with any compost suggested

Frequently Asked Questions About YeoMixes

Q: How can I make YeoMix - JY5 - in an urban kitchen?

A: That is a very good question. So let's make our YeoMix first in kitchen-sized portions.

First, we procure a saucepan and a wheelbarrow.

Or, failing a wheelbarrow, a large kitchen wastebin will serve.

Second, we pour into the wheelbarrow (or wastebin):

10 saucepanfuls (SPFs) of coir (or alternatives that I've suggested above)

6 SPFs of vermiculite or perlite (ditto)
4 SPFs of sand (ditto)
1 SPF of wood ash or charcoal (ditto)
6 SPFs of home-made compost
1 handful of lime (ditto)
1 handful of organic fertiliser - blood meal mixed with bone meal.

That will certainly fill a good-sized wheelbarrow or kitchen wastebin. Now... *mix it all about.*

If you've made it in a wheelie bin, rejoice!

You can now put the lid on, retire to the elderflower lemonade, and forget all about it until - several aeons later - you realise it's time to... *set out your YeoPods.*

But if you've made YeoMix in a wheelbarrow, best make those YeoPods *at once!*

Before your spouse demands his/her wheelbarrow back.

6. Customised Mixes for Specific Plants

To grow greedy potassium feeders...

like tomatoes, squash and other cucurbits, simply double the amount of home-made compost in the YeoMix (**JY5**).

They'll devour fresh compost too, even if only half decomposed. Even fresh kitchen waste. Even farmyard manure a mere three months old.

Even, let it be whispered, *humanure* - fresh from the animal...

Though that is very dangerous and totally *verboten* in the garden, anywhere.

Let's call this rich mix **JY6.**

To grow leafy plants...

like brassica, that need a lot of nitrogen - *double* the amount of blood meal in the mix or add a similar amount of hoof & horn meal.

Or use a high-nitrogen liquid feed. (See Chapter 16.)

Let's call this nitrogenous mix **JY7.**

Why give nitrogen to legumes?

Even legumes need nitrogen... when they're set out.

True, mature legumes *will* 'fix' nitrogen from the air. Textbook writers therefore allege, legumes don't need nitrogen from the soil.

> Suffice to say, my young peas acquired a bad case of *nitrogen chlorosis* - showing yellow 'burnt' lower leaves - when I set out some transplants one year. Solely because my topsoil was nitrogen-deficient.

If you grow legumes in YeoPods, make sure the YeoMix is very well supplied with nitrogen (*as well as* potash - which legumes will need later for pod development)!

Confused, again?

If you've found my plethora of JY mixes above a mite confusing, *relax!* (So did I.)

I will explain them again later in a simplified form in Chapter 14. Then we can *both* understand them.

I will also helpfully include detailed suggestions in Chapter 21 for growing all the most popular garden vegetables in YeoPods.

7. The Neapolitan YeoPod

Much fun can be had by layering a YeoPod like a Neapolitan ice cream, with different mixes at different layers - each adjusted to please the plant at varying stages of its growth.

For example, to grow a plant with a deep taproot, like broccoli or brussel sprouts, a wide GrowCone could first be rammed with a post support.

Then a slim hole might be rammed even deeper within it, with a crow bar.

To keep the slim *lower* hole open for the taproot to descend, we might fill it with a mix of sand, plus our choice of sunflower head crumbs, leaf mould or perlite - for good water retention.

The bottom of the cone itself could comprise wilted nitrogenous nettles, home made compost, topsoil and sand - in roughly equal amounts.

This is a high nitrogen formula!

'Twil be of value to the plant as its roots develop and it starts to develop leaves.

The top of the cone is a gentler mix of compost (or aged crumbled manure), topsoil and perlite (or leaf mould), in roughly equal amounts.

The collar could be filled with a still weaker mix of topsoil, compost and sand in proportions 3:1:1.

The very top layer might simply be a cardboard circle, fitted round the stem of the transplant, or an inch or two of sand, to resist invasion by cabbage root fly, impede evaporation and suppress annual weeds.

The logic of this particular Neopolitan cone is...

that brussel sprouts or broccoli don't need much nutrient in the top soil layer. They need rather more as their leaves grow.

Then they need a *lot* of it - especially nitrogen and potash -

when they're forming buds.

They'll find this as their roots grow into the lower level.

The long taproot - as much as six foot *deep* - can finally snake its way into the lower hole, through any hardpan, then draw upon water in the adjacent subsoil.

Clever, is it not?

Some might argue that brassica - and brussel sprouts in particular - need very firm soil.

Indeed, old textbooks suggest that we *stamp* on the soil with our welly boots. *Or* lay planks on the brassica bed and run a lawn roller over them.

This advice will surprise - and horrify - advocates of 'no dig' gardening who have been successfully growing brussel sprouts and other brassica for years in loose uncompacted soil.

They will aver that 'blown' or ill-formed sprouts (or poor broccoli heads, or cabbages that droop) result simply from poor nutrition. *Not* from loose soil.

I lack the authority to arbitrate in this dispute. I simply know that brussel sprouts grow *wonderfully in* a tall YeoPod, in a nitrogenous - but wholly uncompacted - mix.

Perhaps their roots enjoy pressing against the compacted GrowCone walls?

I only know, *it works.*

To grow large tomatoes...

like beefsteaks, use a similar layered mix - but substitute wilted potash-rich comfrey for nitrogenous nettles, and increase the proportion of compost (or aged manure) at each level.

At the very top, lay an inch of purchased sterile compost, sand or pasteurised topsoil - to stop annual weeds developing.

Of course, this is needlessly complicating YeoPod technology. One joy, among many, of the YeoPod is its foolproof *simplicity*.

Proof? Even *I* can do it.

But these vagrant thoughts do suggest just some of the myriad adventures available to the serious experimenter. Do they not?

A *myriad adventures...*

For example, shall we put raw kitchen waste - or fresh seaweed - at the base of a GrowCone intended for hungry squash plants?

Or a used tea bag, high in potassium, beneath a bean?

Or a phosphorous-rich banana skin, fish head or packet of book matches under a sweet corn plant?

Or mix a spoonful or two of Epsom salts (magnesium sulphate) into a tomato mix, to help the plant distribute calcium and so - arguably - avoid Blossom End Rot?

Or add lime, crushed charcoal or powdered eggshells into the lower level of YeoPods intended for onions or legumes, which dislike acid conditions?

A *scientific test*

To tell whether such alchemy makes a difference, we would need to take several *dozen* identical transplants and insert them into different batches of YeoPods - each filled with a different formula.

For comparison, we would also need a control sample using

just the basic mix.

Fortunately, YeoPods are so easy to make that these trials are feasible in the most modest garden. Whether any result would be *statistically* valid, is irrelevant.

The experiments would yield fun for all... plus revelations!

For example, after due experiment, you might become an apostle of the **FishHead** creed of YeoPod gardening.

You would splinter away from the **TeaBag** sect.

Fierce schism would also arise between you, and advocates of the **BananaPeel** and **BladderWrack** heresies.

You would unite, of course, even with schismatics - to cast out all apostates who dabble in **GrowMore**. *Aroint thee, witch!*

May the joyful experiments begin...

OTHER POTTING MIXES

Truly, your pot mix adventures will be non-ending.

For example, I offer you here the time-tested John Innes recipes, for your playful modification:

Seedling mix

7 parts sterilised loam (humus-rich topsoil)
3 parts shredded leaf mould (John Innes uses moss peat)
2 parts sharp sand

For every eight gallons, add ¾ oz lime (or powdered eggshells) plus 4 oz MiracleGro or a similarly balanced chemical fertiliser.

That comes very close to *John Innes Potting Compost No. 1.*

Mr Innes' other potting mixes are much the same except

that No.2 (for plants potted on) simply has *double* the fertiliser and lime, and No. 3 (for mature plants) has *three* times the fertiliser and lime.

Science is wonderful.

Fortunately, you *won't* need Mr Innes' proprietary chemical additives, if you use the 'all-purpose' YeoMix. Neither will your plants...

Notes

I have included these notes here, merely because I was too lazy to interpolate them earlier. I'm sure you will forgive me.

'Dried' means *thoroughly* dessicated.

Pile the weeds loosely, preferably over a mesh - and turn them regularly, as if you were making hay. Keep them under cover and away from rain.

To chop dry weeds, pile them on a flat surface and run the lawnmower over them a few times. Use only weed leaves and stems. Exclude seed heads.

Leaf mould should be composted for at least a year. However, you can still use part-rotten leaves from many shrubs and trees (provided they are not from acidic conifers), provided you mix in a lot of lime or egg shells to counter the acidity.

Do *not* include lawn clippings.

Even dry, they will heat up and turn your YeoPod into a hot bed.

This may be arguably beneficial in the GrowCone itself - if sunk below early-planted tomatoes, squash and pineapples - but it cannot be generally recommended.

Do *not* use the stems of sunflowers, hollyhocks, jerusalem artichokes or other super-fibrous plants.

Why? They are too woody to be a good coir replacement

(unless totally pulverised). They are far better used, shredded - as free organic replacements for vermiculite or perlite.

Or they can be placed at the bottom of conventional large flower pots to improve drainage.

At season's end, they'll be rotten and the entire contents of your tubs or flower pots can be safely tossed onto your garden, without the nuisance of having to sift out the hydroleca, gravel, broken crocks, polybeads or other non-degradeable detritus you placed there for drainage.

Or have I, uh, *said that before?*

Chapter 14

The YeoPod Formulae

Here are formulae for the home-made potting mixes suggested for each plant in chapter 21 - The Plant Cornucopia.

Please feel free to experiment with alternative ingredients.

JY4 and JY2 are interchangeable for most purposes, as are JY3, JY6 and JY3A. Their choice will depend on the ingredients you have most easily to hand.

In extremis, *any* of the 'all-purpose' mixes - JY2, JY4 and JY5 - will serve well enough for most plants, in both cone and collar.

JY1 - a light mix for carrots, parsnips and other roots

1 pailful coir
1 pailful sharp sand
1 pailful aged leaf mould
1 pailful sieved topsoil
1 pailful vermiculite or perlite
2 cups of a mix of blood meal, bone meal and wood ashes in equal proportions
1 cup lime (if topsoil is acidic)
½ pailful powdered charcoal (optional)

Note: if using this as a seedling mix, omit the blood and bone meal.

JY2 - an all-purpose mix

2 parts purchased compost
1 part sieved topsoil
1 part sharp sand

JY3 - a rich mix

2 parts purchased compost
1 part sieved topsoil
1 part sieved aged cow manure (or any farm manure except poultry manure), or aged seaweed

JY3A - a very rich mix

1 part sieved well rotted manure (or aged seaweed)
1 part sieved home made compost
1 part aged leafmould
½ part sharp sand

JY4 - an all-purpose mix

2 gallons sieved topsoil
2 gallons aged leafmould
2 gallons home-made compost, aged manure or rotted seaweed
1 cup bonemeal
2 cups seaweed meal
½ cup calcified seaweed, ground limestone or dolomite (if topsoil is acidic)

JY5 - the all-purpose YeoMix

10 parts coir
6 parts vermiculite or perlite
4 parts sharp sand
1 part woodash and/or charcoal
8 parts home-made compost
1/20th part lime or powdered eggshells
1/20th part bone meal mixed equally with blood meal

JY6 - a very rich mix

As JY5, but using 16 parts compost or 8 parts compost plus 8 parts aged manure

JY7 - a nitrogenous mix eg. for brassica

As JY5, but using twice as much (ie. 1/10th) part blood meal or hoof and horn meal.

Note: when sieving these mixes for cones or collars use nothing smaller than a ½ inch mesh. Too fine a mix may become compacted.

Chapter 15

The simplest way to make compost

Compost is, to the organic gardener, what bread and ale were to William Cobbett's yeomen of olde England - no good unless home made.

Indeed, to buy either was, to Cobbett, a sinful admission of sloth, folly and bad husbandry.

What you could so easily bake or brew in your own kitchen was, he pointed out, not only cheaper but... more nutritious and less likely to be adulterated.

His argument holds good today.

To buy 240 litres of multi-purpose compost at a garden centre, a person earning a minimum wage would, after paying taxes, have to labour for three hours.

Yet much the same quantity of compost could be made at home in a total period of around 30 minutes, consisting merely of 15 weekly two-minute trips to the compost heap with a bucket of lawn clippings or smelly rubbish.

If your compost heap is more than two minutes' walk away, your garden is enormous and probably owned by the National Trust. So you can borrow *their* gardener to empty your kitchen waste.

> This reduces your manhours still further and strengthens my argument.

Moreover, make your own compost and you have the comfort of knowing exactly... *what's in it.* With care, you can produce a consistent, precisely balanced and top-quality product.

Beware shop-bought compost

Shop-bought compost is *not* necessarily superior to home-made; indeed, quite the reverse. Independent trials by *Gardening Which?* in the UK showed dramatic differences in growing results between different brands.

Some brands were so deficient in nitrogen they actually *suppressed* plant growth.

This was especially true of peat-free formulations for seedlings.

There are no regulated standards in the UK, at time of writing, for compost quality.

Even the basic components of purchased compost are rarely declared on the bag, let alone their chemical balance (though manufacturers *will* divulge such details, if you persist). Also, unless you specify an organic blend, it will be laced with chemical fertiliser.

For example, the only significant differences between John Innes #1, #2 and #3 potting composts are... the amount of chemical fertiliser and chalk or lime included!

The main virtue of shop-bought compost...

apart from convenience, is its fine crumbly texture. But a fine texture is only important for seed trays. And *all* compost - even purchased 'potting mix' - is far too rich for seedlings anyway. (For better mixes, see Chapter 13.)

Of course, at the outset you may have no alternative to shop-bought. At least, it's sterile - so it makes a good weed-suppressing mulch in a YeoPod.

But 'twould be wise to start a compost bin as soon as possible.

Please be reassured, I will *not* require you to nail together four discarded pallets. Or, in the Southern hemisphere, hinge together four flyscreen doors.

Or recycle a rabbit hutch, dog kennel, coal bunker, garden incinerator, child's Wendy house, chest freezer, builder's rubble sack or several tractor tyres (stacked to dizzying heights), as recommended by certain gardening gurus.

Such expedients may indeed make excellent compost... and enhance your reputation as a wise eccentric.

   An eccentric is a gardener who lacks the energy to become a crank.

But they are ugly.

Nor do you need to dig a four foot *deep* hole in the garden (and every year hire a mini-excavator to retrieve its contents).

Nor buy, at unspeakable cost, a barrel mounted on sprockets and gears that must be turned daily by a crank.

   Anything that must be turned by a crank, I find, usually is.

Instead, I have at no small effort devised for you the perfect home compost maker that demands of you no effort at all. Clean, hygienic and always close to hand. You can keep it in your patio or drive.

In fact, those are the *best* places to keep a compost bin. The more sun it gets, the faster it works.

Moreover, it's pretty.

How to make perfect compost in a YeoBin

First, procure a tall plastic laundry basket or, failing that, a large vertical kitchen waste bin. In either case, the lid is optional. Many bins can be found free at council recycling yards or discarded in beauty spots.

A giant plastic dustbin or wheelie bin makes an ideal YeoBin but it must be well hidden. Or your waste collection service will helpfully empty it every week.

A big water butt is a *wonderful* option, especially if it leaks and is otherwise useless.

A tall laundry basket - inserted within a large water butt or garbage can - is a counsel of perfection!

It has ample ventilation, insulation and weather protection. Best of all, it promotes marital felicity because, with luck, your spouse - once you have borrowed it - *will never find it again...*

Drill ¼ inch ventilation holes lavishly around the sides of the bin. Laundry baskets are usually too well perforated already. In that case, mask the holes inside with a roll of old carpet to keep waste in and rodents and scavenging birds out.

You won't need to do that, of course, if your laundry basket is hidden within a water butt or garbage can.

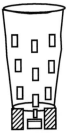

Second, drill a large single hole in the base, and set the bin on bricks with a dish beneath the hole. Conventional bins are sadly deficient in this technical feature.

It prevents liquid collecting, turning acidic at the base and killing the beneficial micro-organisms. Any nutritious fluid that drips out can also be diluted for immediate use as a plant food.

It's super-rich...

That's why the soil beneath any conventional bin, one built on bare earth, is super-rich and can itself be used in place of compost.

The drainage hole is optional but, if you don't have one, lay a couple of inches of soil or crumpled or shredded cardboard at the base. This soaks up the effluvia, which might otherwise become acidic.

Third, build the bin in alternate layers with (a)
kitchen waste, (b) lawn clippings or other
fresh leafy matter - plus (c) crumpled
cardboard.

Cardboard is vital

The cardboard is vital because it introduces air. Using
cardboard, you can avoid all need thereafter to mix or turn
the materials in the bin.

> This is just as well. Folk rarely *do* turn their heaps anyway and, in a
> kitchen waste bin, it's impossible.

Crushed toilet rolls and cereal packets are admirable.
Fragments of corrugated packing cases are okay.
Newspaper is fine too, but *only* if shredded or crunched into
small tight balls. Flat slabs of it will *not* rot down.

> An entire edition of the *Daily Mail* that I used to interleave one
> compost heap was still perfectly readable two years later. That
> delayed my bin turning efforts. Because, of course, *I had to read every*
> *word...*

Newspapers are less toxic than your garden

Incidentally, the printing inks used on newspapers today -
black or coloured - are largely soy-based and are safe in a
compost heap. Research at the UK's Centre for Alternative
Technology has shown that levels of toxic metals present in
newspapers are actually *lower* than those in average garden
soil.

But coloured glossy magazines are still best avoided.

> They also take ages to rot down

Each layer should be no more than two inches deep. Purists
might also scatter lime or crushed eggshells every two or
three layers as a further precaution against the bin

growing acidic.

But I will not insist...

But that is starting to sound like **Work,** so I will not insist.

Lime helpfully lowers acidity in the bin, which promotes compost-forming bacteria. But it *also* reduces available nitrogen, which slows the compost-forming process.

Confused? Just let's agree, *lime is optional...*

Unless your lawn clippings or kitchen waste are wet to start with, sprinkle a cupful of water at every level. The bin will heat up faster if you cover it with a carpet or old dog blanket (which also deters cats).

> But this is not essential - provided you have a drainage hole in the bottom to vent rainstorms.

Fourth, set the bin within easy walking distance of your kitchen door. Collect the kitchen scraps in a sealed bucket indoors then, whenever your nose (or spouse) insists, dump them in the YeoBin.

Textbooks say a compost heap must be at least one yard (okay, one metre) wide, long and *deep* before it gains enough critical mass to heat up. To be sure of killing weed seeds and diseases - eg. from blighted potato haulm - the heap must sustain a temperature of around 150°F for several days.

That is hot!

It is close to the temperature of an Aga, in its bottom oven (with its door open). If you withdraw a crowbar that's been in a 150°F heap, you will not be able to hold it.

You can fry an egg, cook porridge, bake a chicken or stew a

casserole at the heap's core. And so save on your fuel bills.

It's true. I once stewed some 10-year old soy beans in stock for three days in a sealed casserole dish at the heart of a compost heap. Tender and delicious they were. But nobody else would sample them...

will your bin get that hot?

A large 80 gallon water butt in Summer might well do so and you can encourage a heap to 'work' by sprinkling on any animal or poultry manure (but never dog, cat or human faeces), dilute urine or a nitrogenous solution of Phostrogen or Growmore.

The latter will horrify organic gardeners, of course. Yet I see no harm in using a trivial amount of chemical nitrogen to kickstart an otherwise organic compost heap. Unless, of course, you have an ethical objection to subsidising chemical companies.

But probably the smaller bins will *not* get that hot. It doesn't matter. You'll still get compost. You'll simply get it a little later.

Our purpose here is *not* to kill diseases or weeds - but to make compost. So just keep diseased plant waste, weed roots and seedheads *out* of the bin and you'll have no problem.

Frequently Asked Questions about YeoBins

Question: Suppose I have no lawn, therefore no lawn clippings?

Answer: No matter. A mixture of kitchen waste and crumpled cardboard will, by itself, produce usable compost. Nitrogenous lawn clippings - or stinging nettles or comfrey stems and leaves - simply accelerate the process and add nutrients.

Perhaps neighbours can save their lawn clippings for you?

Just be sure they haven't sprayed it with weed suppressant chemicals in recent weeks.

> Anything that kills clover or creeping buttercup will do your vegetables, or you, no good at all.

If they've merely raked in a nitrogenous lawn fertiliser (the kind with no toxic additives), the clippings are fine. But be advised... *you have crazy neighbours*. Best move house.

Fertilising the lawn will simply force them to mow it, and so ruin your weekend siestas, twice as often as necessary.

Question: Suppose I mix in soil?

Answer: A little topsoil is a good thing. It introduces innoculants, which kickstart the compost bacteria. It can be laid at the base of the bin or layered between kitchen waste to reduce any odour.

But enough soil will be introduced anyway on the roots of any weeds you compost. If you don't get it by accident, don't worry about it.

Question: Suppose I can't muster enough kitchen waste?

Answer: Even a large family of veggie eaters will be hard pressed to fill a bin with their own vegetable trimmings alone. In fact, a well balanced heap is never full.

> So fast will your garbage shrink in warm weather that you'll swear somebody is stealing it.

One solution is to scour local independent greengrocers and farm shops and beg for their throwaways. Say candidly, you're an organic grower and are setting up a recycling round for compostable waste.

Most will be truly grateful if, every week, you relieve them of the chore of disposing of veggies that are past their 'sell by' date.

> Let it be whispered, many such a vegetable is still perfectly good to eat...

Leave your own plastic wastebin at a restaurant, fish and chip shop - or a pub with a brisk catering trade - and ask them to fill it with vegetable trimmings.

Uplift it every week. Even those misguided places that, increasingly today, serve 'cryovac' food boiled in bags may still have enough conscience to use - and peel - at least, fresh vegetables...

Just one outlet like this will give you more kitchen waste than you can ever handle, for one small bin.

> Especially if you give them a basket of home-grown vegetables now and again.

So you'll have to start several *more* bins!

> No, I will *not* suggest you put your kitchen waste first through a heavy-duty kitchen blender, or sink disposal unit - so it rots down in mere days. Environmentalists will rightly pillory me, for proposing such a gross misuse of energy.

Question: Suppose I want to compost other forms of waste?

Answer: I am sure you are a serious gardener or you would not be reading this book. So you need no counsel from me in what to put *in* a compost bin, and what to exclude.

Suffice to say, there is *nothing* wrong in putting meat or fish waste in a bin. Whatever the textbooks say. It will compost down as well as anything else that has ever lived.

But next day... the bin will be scattered all over your garden by cats, large birds and rats.

> Is this what they call 'sheet mulching'?

Best stick to vegetable waste, raw or cooked.

Contrary to myth, most leaves are also fine.

But steer clear of oak, chestnut, beech, pine (and other conifer) leaves. They compost slowly, make the heap acidic and decompose by fungal rather than bacterial action. A fungal compost that has decomposed in this way is good for trees and shrubs but *not* ideal for vegetables.

A small amount of even acidic leaves are okay, however, *if* you mix them with lime or powdered egg shells.

Or if you love work, you could shred acidic leaves so they decompose quickly - by dunking them in a barrel and working them around with a powerful garden strimmer.

Question: Suppose I want to save compost for next year?

Answer: It's true that the best compost is that which comes straight from a cooled heap, at the time when the worms and wood lice (pillbugs) are just moving in. The micro-organisms beneficial to soil health are then at their peak.

> Professional growers rightly insist on fresh compost each year.

But if you have too much compost, don't let it sit in the bin. Transfer it to plastic manure bags or the like, and keep in a dry cool place, and it will still be full enough of nutrients next year. Then you can refill the empty bins...

Question: How do I get the compost *out* of a YeoBin?

Answer: Sorry. I'd forgotten to mention that.

Well, you lay a large piece of plastic or tarpaulin in front of the bin and... just tip the bin over. This is very easy if you use a wheelie bin.

It's even easier if you ask the postman to do it.

> A well cultivated postman is a garden asset and can be readily motivated by an annual bottle of scotch.

In fact, if you are on good terms with your council rubbish collectors they might agree to uplift your wheelie bin every week, its lid firmly tied on, give it a little shake on the back of their lorry - and return it to you still full.

This mixing process will indisputably accelerate compost production.

> On reflection, better not. Some jobsworth will then knock on your door... to check... if you are making proper use of the council's wheelie bin.

If you want to make compost even more easily...

(some people are never satisfied), simply fill a strong big plastic bag - like an empty manure sack - with the layers I suggest above. Tie it loosely at the top, so gases can escape. And leave it in a warm place.

Even your bathroom.

The compost process will then proceed *anaerobically* (without oxygen), be fairly odourless and take a lot longer. But in hot weather, you may still have compost - albeit with the slimey texture of fresh cow manure - within three months.

The great value

One great value of 'plastic bag' compost is that you can periodically kick the bag around your courtyard, thus mixing the ingredients.

This also works off any resentment you might feel upon discovering that your spouse has, after all, retrieved the laundry basket...

What's more, when the compost is done (ie. it smells more wholesome than your spouse) you need merely toss in a few spadefuls of topsoil, plus perhaps a little sand.

Kick the bag around the garden a bit more to mix its contents, perforate one side and cut holes in the other side, and...

you have a Tomato GrowBag!

Chapter 16

Free liquid feeds for your YeoPods

Let's take a break from YeoPods for a moment.

With your permission, I will instead consider the perfidy of chemical fertiliser companies.

Chemical fertiliser is a giant industry with a large advertising budget. So it's not surprising that the most popular gardening magazines urge us to dowse our gardens with a cocktail of soil amendments every Spring.

But what *is* surprising is... most gardens with even half-way decent soil need *no fertiliser at all.*

True, the vegetable patch may need renourishing each year, but only because of the amount of food we take out of it.

A one inch top dressing of compost every Autumn (plus perhaps a little bone and blood meal), which the worms obligingly drag down for us, is usually more than enough to sustain fertility.

You don't even need much compost.

A typical three cubic foot bag of home made compost, same as an 80 litre bag of purchased compost, will cover 36 sq ft - say, a typical bed four foot by nine foot - one inch deep. That's adequate.

So it's only worth risking your back to dig in tons of manure each season *if...* you badly need to improve the soil texture.

> For example, heavy clay or fine sandy soils may call for a lot of manure or other organic matter, to improve drainage or water retention. Respectively.

Much of the nitrogen in manure is leached out of the soil over Winter, anyway. Best to add it in early Spring.

Even fresh leaves or sawdust can be dug in, though gardening veterans will point out this impoverishes the soil.

And they're right. It's a good preliminary to sowing wildflowers, which flower *only* in poor nitrogen-deficient soil.

But it works fine if...

you mix the leaves or sawdust with a lot of animal manure to replace the nitrogen lost while they decay (and to speed their decay) plus - several months later - lime or powdered eggshells to counter acidity.

Just don't plant anything there for, say, six months?

That said, it's far less work to dig or hoe shallow trenches, fill them with kitchen waste, lightly cover with soil - and walk away. Keep digging and filling those trenches, week by week, at staggered locations for a year or five. And you've done the job.

Or rather, the worms - attracted to that newly fertile soil - will do the job for you.

If you're really lazy...

just spread a lot of kitchen waste continuously on the soil, cover it with topsoil to hide the smell - and be prepared to wait a year or two.

Of course, if you habitually make *enough* YeoPods even the worse ground will be improved much sooner than that - by the good soil you've imported. *Plus* the drainage holes left by rotting plant roots in the YeoPods.

Your back will bless you.

Did I say digging?

If done from habit rather than necessity (say, to improve soil texture or to make a planting hole in stony ground), digging can actually *harm* the soil - by releasing carbon dioxide and upsetting the balance of mycorrhiza, both of which benefit plant roots.

It also propagates zillions of weed seeds by exposing them to air and light, as you'll soon discover if you do it.

> Plowing is even *worse*. Witness the arid wastes of East Anglia - Britain's own Saharan desert, created over the last 50 years by over-plowing plus the manic use of chemical fertiliser.

Chemical fertiliser?

It has much the same effect on the soil as over-digging. It destroys mycorrhiza. So double digging in your garden, then adding Growmore and lime every year as some textbooks advise, but never adding organic matter... is the route to eventual soil sterility.

Fertiliser also works most quickly on the fastest growing plants - weeds. So the more we fertilise, *the bigger our weed problems*.

Even liming can be overdone.

Soil may indeed need lime or wood ash at the outset to correct acidity but, if the plants are systematically returned to the garden by way of the compost heap, the garden retains its lime.

> So to lime very much thereafter - or add wood ash - should be unnecessary.

True, I lack the qualifications to make such assertions. I merely report the research of many soil scientists over several decades. To them, I am profoundly grateful because... I hate double digging (and, having a back problem, I can't do it anyway)...

Our worst-case scenario

All this 'lazy gardening' advice may be arguably true of the average garden but, remember? We have a worst-case scenario. We start with utterly bleak soil. Rocky, compacted, hard-panned, intractible, infertile or weed-infested...

> Of course, if a soil is infested with weeds it can hardly be called infertile. But you get my drift. Regardless, that soil is *awful...*

Fortunately, we are now equipped with... YeoPods!

Filling a YeoPod with the ideal growing mix for every plant will get the plants very well established.

If the surrounding soil is only moderately awful, most plants - even climbing legumes - will need nothing more. So my following advice is intended for those - only - who have special needs.

Special needs?

A large fruiting plant like a squash or indeterminate tomato (especially a beefsteak) will exhaust the nutrients in a YeoPod in around six to eight weeks from planting out.

To get the maximum yield of fruit, the plant will then need nourishment from elsewhere. If the adjacent soil cannot provide this, supplementary liquid feeding - by organic means - may be necessary.

Liquid plant foods (emergency)

Many and unlikely are the liquid plant foods that can give plants a temporary - or emergency - boost.

Fish water from a fish-filled aquarium or garden pond is rich in nitrogen so might benefit brassica and other leafy plants, for a time.

So will a packet of nitrogenous **gelatine** dissolved in a

quart of warm water.

A solution of **wood ash** or even ash from your grate (provided it contains no more than 25% coal ash) gives a little phosphorous plus a lot of instant potassium.

But these expedients lack other nutrients.

The rinse water from **sprouted seeds** is full of plant growth hormones, it's said. So pour it on seedlings and young plants.

The mineral-rich water in which vegetables have **boiled** is more nutritious than rain water, and especially tap water - but not dramatically so. It's worth pouring on house plants but I wouldn't bother trekking it down the garden...

Some folk even attest to human **urine**, diluted one part to five parts water, as a corrective to nitrogen deficiency.

Let it be whispered, the urine from a pre-menopausal woman is said to be rich in hormones that will unspeakably boost the growth of young plants. *But I will not pursue this topic further...*

Needless to say, you may be reluctant to eat vegetables nourished by urine.

Cold **tea** is a fabled plant restorative.

Why? It contains *triacontanel* which stimulates plant growth. (I knew you'd ask...)

Old tea bags can also be infused in cold water for a week to yield a mild plant pick-me-up. But, for a full nutrient balance, they can't compete with the *Power House* formulae (see below).

The water that **eggs** have boiled in contains calcium. So folk have theorised it should prevent *Blossom End Rot* (BER) in tomatoes.

However, BER has little to do with calcium-deficiency in

the soil itself. It is all about a stressed plant being unable to circulate the calcium already amply available to it. So this is a worthless urban (sorry, *rural*) myth.

Powdered **kelp** from a health food shop contains a fabulous array of trace minerals - potash, magnesium, manganese, zinc, plus just about everything else.

A kelp infusion of 1 heaped tablespoon per gallon of rain water, mixed and left for just one hour, will get new transplants off to a good start.

Spray it on the seedlings and it works as a fungicide to deter damping off disease, too.

It will reliably correct most mineral deficiencies thereafter, even in mature plants.

But kelp has little nitrogen. It is also expensive unless bought in bulk from a wholesaler.

Kept in dark sealed jars, it stores well and is then a fabulous investment, I find. It will profit you for many years.

A cheaper alternative to kelp (dried powdered seaweed) is *fresh* **seaweed** (see later).

Potent alternatives

It cannot be denied, other liquid foods may be just as potent as the five *Power House* foods below.

For example, **borage** contains so much nitrogen that the dried leaves were once used as touchpaper for fireworks (I'm told). So I'm sure brassica would love a weekly infusion of borage.

Bracken is so rich in potash it was once a major industrial source of potassium.

You can mulch any fruiting plant with six inches of wilted bracken, to its advantage. *Or* pour a bracken infusion on your tomatoes, beans and cucurbits when they start to fruit.

Relax. Whatever you've heard, bracken is *not* carcinogenic.

Only the spores might be, and bracken sporulates only rarely, and then only in Spring. Infusing - or composting - the plant avoids any potential problem. *Or so I read...*

Chickweed rivals even comfrey, for all-round nutrients. (Pour its infusion anywhere.)

> Other weeds especially rich in minerals include thistles, dandelions, rose bay willow herb and cow parsley.

Soot is high in nitrogen, plus sulphur. That's probably why a soot infusion - or a sulphur-rich garlic infusion - is an effective foliar spray against powdery mildew and other moulds, such as botrytis.

Slosh it on your pea roots, then spray it on the pea leaves - both top and bottom surfaces. Do it at once if the mature leaves are inexplicably becoming yellow (*nitrogen chlorosis*) or, worse, powdery and white (*Powdery mildew*).

How to make an infusion

Any of the materials above, including the *Power House* ingredients below, can be infused in a tub of water for several weeks (the soot being contained in a cloth bag like a pillow case).

> If you lack a big enough bucket or barrel, use an impermeable plastic manure bag or a tough refuse sack, tied loosely at the top.

The liquid is then strained. (Use several layers of cheesecloth or muslin if you intend to spray it as a foliar spray, or it will clog the spray.) The residue is tossed on the compost heap.

Any surplus can be frozen in plastic milk or cola bottles and re-used next year.

Do label it well, or you'll be pouring it into a casserole by mistake. I
speak from experience...

True, freezing an infusion will kill the beneficial
microorganisms which pullulate in fresh manure, compost
or comfrey tea, and which make them so valuable eg. as
fungal deterrents. But sterile purchased compost doesn't
contain live microorganisms either, and - after a fashion - it
does its job.

The fluid is then diluted according to the type, or maturity,
of the plant you're going to pour it on.

Recommended dilutions

One part infusion to five parts water is recommended for
well-established plants, especially when fruiting.

> One to ten is for brassica. One to 20 is for all other
> plants. And one to 40 is for very young plants.

You can usually pour a strong infusion - one to five - on
well-established onions, brassica, strawberries, cucurbits,
sweet corn and tomatoes every week, without harm.

But because nobody can judge the strength of your
infusion, or the tolerance of your plants, experiment and
common sense must be your guides.

In moderation, be extreme....

Alas, few of the materials above are available to gardeners
in volume. So we must resort to other options. Fortunately,
most of them are even better.

The five Power House infusions

The five most reliable and potent sources of organic liquid
fertiliser are comfrey, nettles, animal or poultry manure,
compost and - if you're lucky enough to live near a clean
beach - seaweed.

All have the advantage of being free and at least one should be abundant, no matter where you live.

Each has its own nutritional strengths, as you'll see from the **Table** in the next Chapter.

Comfrey is fabled for potash (potassium), nettles for nitrogen, poultry manure for nitrogen and phosphorous, compost for everything, and seaweed for potash plus trace nutrients.

But, of course, this is overly simplistic.

For example, the **Green Thumb Rule** tells us that root vegetables need phosphorous, leaf vegetables demand nitrogen and fruiting vegetables require potash.

So, if we try to be scientific, we might specify a poultry manure infusion on carrots, nettle tea on brassica and comfrey feed on tomatoes.

But plants themselves are not that simplistic.

Pour poultry manure tea on carrots, for example, and - while it may contain a lot of phosphorous - the carrots won't like it. The massive nitrogen content may cause them to fork.

However, carrots might indeed do well if given a wood ash infusion, which gently adds phosphorous and potassium without nitrogen.

Legumes like beans and peas will likewise enjoy the potassium in wood ash. Won't they? *No, they wont.*

When I grew two identical rows, one with wood ash at the base and the other not, the unfertilised beans did a massive *70%* better in terms of crop yield than those with wood ash.

Is that because young beans and peas in their early weeks

need - not potash - but far more nitrogen than they can 'fix' for themselves from the air?

So is this the best time to pour on nitrogen-rich nettle tea?

And do they welcome potash, such as from wood ash, *only* when... they're forming blossom and fruits?

Frankly, I don't know. The good news is... *nobody else really knows either!*

That's one of the joys of experimental gardening. You and I, serious gardeners, are just as likely to come up with a valid fresh insight as any plant scientist.

At least, legumes have no problems, I find, ingesting the nitrogen and high potassium - in **seaweed** extract.

To compound our confusion, the nutritional needs of each species will also change at different *stages* of growth. And under different *growing* conditions.

So let's not get too scientific...

Plant scientists may be happy to match a particular type of feed to a particular species. Or to switch energetically - as hydroponicists do - between different types and strengths of feed a half dozen times, as the plants mature.

For us home growers, it's far easier to use just one type of feed, based on what we have readily to hand, that's already well balanced in all three of the essential nutrients.

Okay, some exceptions *might* include tomatoes and cucurbits - that appreciate a high potash feed as they are setting fruit, and leafy vegetables which respond well to nitrogenous nettle tea, just as they are forming hearts or buds.

Mix and match

For the best balanced nutrient tea, mix several components together.

For example, comfrey (potash) and nettles (nitrogen) complement each other. Or you could throw in almost any garden weed you have to hand - the more different they are in terms of family, the better.

Each weed adds its own unique blend of trace nutrients.

Even the most virulent weeds like bindweed, marestail, couch grass, seeding dock or creeping buttercup - which you dare not toss on the hottest compost heap lest their roots and seeds survive - can be rotted under water for four weeks.

The roots and seeds are then harmless and the brew will be full of nutrients.

> Indeed, I once founded a small cottage industry, by rotting my pestilential marestail in water. I then poured that silica-rich infusion as a plant food on my tomatoes and sweet corn and sprayed it on legumes and squash to deter powdery mildew.
>
> I also sold dried powdered marestail to other organic growers, for those purposes.
>
> No, it did not make me rich. But I was delightfully reminded me of the adage "if life hands you a lemon, *make lemonade...*"

Lawn clippings are a rich nitrogen source. A cocktail of mixed weeds and grass (if free of chemicals) is very palatable to plants, being rich in most nutrients.

> Grass, like marestail, is also saturated with silica. Herbivores like cows and horses have special teeth to cope with silica whereas, if we chewed grass all day, our teeth would become stubs. Plants, however, need silica to resist disease and pests. *Pour it on...*

Have fun compounding your own balanced brews.

This one **TigerBrew** combines potassium, phosphorous, nitrogen and a vast range of trace minerals and nutrients.

    1 part fish emulsion
    2 parts powdered kelp

10 parts dried cow manure
50 parts water

If you use wet cow manure, increase its quantity by one third.

Let the mix stand in a covered container for a day.

How to make your own fish emulsion

If you have no sense of smell but access to lots of fish
scraps - and I know several beach-living members of the
Village Guild - try this recipe.

Cover fish scraps with water in a sealed bucket for
three months. Holding your nose, skim off the top layer
of oil and compost the residue.

It's highly nitrogenous, will kickstart your compost heap and - unless
in a sealed bin - give your local rats a feast day.

Dilute the oil 1:80 in water as a nitrogenous root feed.
Or use it - neat and undiluted - in the recipe above.

The oil will store in a sealed jar in the fridge for several
months.

But beware: like buffalo cheese, no matter how
tightly you seal the jar, *that awful smell will leak out...*

Back to the TigerBrew

Most fruiting or seed-producing plants will love this elixir,
especially when they are about to form fruit. Pour it over
their roots, ideally just before a heavy rain so the roots will
be well saturated in it.

That brew is *powerful!*

So use it cautiously at first to see how the plant responds.
Restrict it also to mature plants with well-established root
systems. Frankly, so much nitrogen will kill seedlings and
can spur young plants, all too quickly, into over-lush

growth...

If you pour it on acid-loving plants like strawberries, add one teaspoon of cider vinegar per pint. Now it's an *ericaceous* brew!

> That also might be a good idea for feeding potatoes and berry fruit. Even heathers and rhodedondrons... if you're eccentric enough to grow non-edible plants, that is.

Comfrey

If you're a passionate organic gardener, you already have a battalion of comfrey plants. They muster at the back of your garden, ready to give you - on demand - instant free fertiliser.

Instant? Lay a few fresh comfrey leaves in the planting hole of almost any plant - especially sweet corn, tomatoes, beans, peas and cucurbits - and the plant will show its appreciation in mere days.

> Comfrey is nearly as rich as banana peel in nitrogen and potash.

Comfrey is - by dry weight - higher in phosphorous and potash than cow manure, nettles or compost. It's the workhorse of the organic garden.

Plant it around mint or creeping elder, and it will contain them. Spray comfrey infusion on any plant subject to fungal disease or mould, and it will suppress the mould.

Slosh it on your carrots, and carrot fly won't go near them. It's said...

Eat it

You can also, deliciously, *eat* the leaves, stems and flowers - in any recipe that might work for spinach or collard leaves, or cucurbit flowers. Just be prepared for the comfrey, like nettle leaves, to reduce enormously in cooking. Youll need a *lot!*

> No, comfrey is *not* significantly carcinogenic, despite scare stories you might have read. Only the roots might be unhealthy to eat and then only if you eat vast quantities. And you *won't*, will you?

> You can also put comfrey poultices on burns or fractures. And it works... My arms are as clear as a baby's bottom, although we have a burn-promoting Aga cooker. That's because I slap a comfrey leaf on every burn as it happens.

You can see... comfrey is a **Good Thing.**

where do you get comfrey?

You'll find it by almost any UK roadside.

Technically, it's illegal in the UK to dig up roots from the wilds and transplant them to your garden - even though dividing a few comfrey roots will not harm the parent plant and, indeed, will ensure its survival.

> Just like dividing rhubarb roots, in fact...

Even roadside roots that are saturated with lead from petrol, will yield - when transplanted - fresh leaves which are perfectly safe to compost or infuse as a plant food.

> I concede, the law - in this rare case - does make sense. For example, cowslip was once abundant in the UK as a common 'weed' till folk started transplanting it to their gardens. Now it's a rare and endangered species in the wild.

But you can get comfrey, legally, from many a private ground and your neighbours may even pay you to dig it out for them. Just a few root fragments will fill your garden within a year.

> **A tip:** bury the root fragments *sideways*. Then you get twice the growth. That tip also works with horseradish and dandelion roots.

Or you can buy seed from herbal plant suppliers. (My 500

sq yards of comfrey were mostly grown from seed.)

A tip: wild comfrey is invasive. It sets new growth vigorously by both root and seed. Russian comfrey does *not* set seed, and is less invasive. And a special strain Bocking 14 from the UK's HDRA does not set seed or invade at all, and is also richer in plant nutrients.

Did you know there exist as many as 20 unique Bocking comfrey variations - from 1 unto 20? But 14 is the best. (Few folk but you and I know that.)

Personally, I *want* comfrey to invade my garden.

It looks very decorative among my wife's flowers, and attracts bees. If necessary, I can easily kill it.

Get the whole root out, and - unlike marestail - *it won't come back.*

I can eat it, use it for fertiliser and medicine, and even make a hair shampoo out of it.

I love comfrey!

To make comfrey tea

Comfrey calls for slightly different treatment from the standard infusion method (above).

So succulent are its stems and leaves, you can just pack them down in a tub without water.

They'll deliquesce into a rich brown liqueur in three weeks (subject to temperature), all by themselves.

Even so, I still like to add a little water. Not least, because I always mix comfrey with nettles to balance the nutrients. And without water, nettles - like most other fibrous weeds - don't rot. They turn into straw.

Adventurers have crafted **Comfrey Pipes**.

They have taken an eight inch diameter plastic sewer pipe, around five foot long. They have capped off the top and

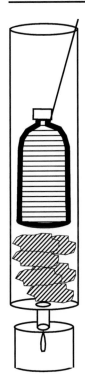

bottom, and drilled a hole in the base. They have lashed that tube to a pole. They have put a bottle below the hole.

They have then packed the pipe with comfrey stems and leaves. They have filled a plastic cola bottle (or a champagne bottle) with water.

They have tied that heavy weight at the neck and dropped it on top of the comfrey.

In due course, they have been gratified as brown smelly comfrey elixir drips out into their bottle.

I salute those Adventurers! Not least, because it reassures me to know that some folk are (unbelievably) even more eccentric than I am.

No, you do *not* need a Comfrey Pipe. A simple bucket or plastic bag will suffice. And be a lot less work...

You can cut a mature comfrey plant up to five times a year without weakening it. To increase your stock, simply divide the roots in Autumn. Even small fragments will grow into a new plant.

Nettles

Both stinging nettles *(Urticas)* and dead nettles *(Lamiums)* are high in nitrogen and potash and can be infused into a nutritious tea.

Half fill a tub with the leaves and stems, top up with rain water and leave for a few weeks.

Cucurbits in particular are said to thrive on nettle tea in

the early weeks when they're forming leaves and need nitrogen.

Why are comfrey and nettle infusions so beneficial to plants?

It's still an open question. Their nutrient levels are relatively low compared with chemical fertilisers, like MiracleGro or Phostrogen.

Yet when attempts have been made to replicate their nutrients using chemicals... plants fed on the organic brews have outperformed those grown on the chemical equivalents.

Doubtless, the chemical brews lacked the live microorganisms found in the organic feed. So the fresher the organic brew, the more valuable it will be.

Manure

Any farmyard manure, wet or dry, can be infused into a nitrogen-rich feed.

> The important exceptions are cat, dog and human faeces which contain pathogens. They should not be used even on flower beds. The pathogens can still be ingested accidentally, or brushed on the eyes, if transmitted by hands or feet. And children *have* become blind.

Even in cities you can usually get manure. Seek out local rabbit, pigeon or poultry clubs. Or follow a circus around.

Poultry manure tops the farmyard league for nitrogen.

So fierce is it that, if used on the soil, it should be laid in Autumn to age over Winter and never scattered close to growing plants.

Rabbit or guinea pig manures are more benign and, well mixed with straw, make a useful mulch for nitrogen-loving plants.

In an infusion, however, even bat guano - which has up to

19% nitrogen, higher than pigeon droppings, and is rarely seen today - will infuse into a safe feed if the liquor is well diluted.

The PillowCase TeaPot

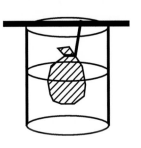

Fill a pillow case or hessian (burlap) sack with manure and suspend it in a tub of water, agitating occasionally, for about a month.

The sack makes it easy to strain.

The manure that's left over can be laid on the compost heap, and will help activate it.

The TeaPot Ensuite

A lazy way to nourish gross feeders like squash is to cut the bottom off a plastic cola or milk bottle. Screw on its cap. Perforate the neck.

Sink that funnel beside the plants when they're set out. When time comes to feed the plant, half fill the bottle with manure and top it up periodically with water.

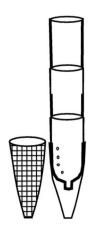

That method works well with YeoPods and there's no need to dig a hole.

Simply ram in *two* GrowCones side by side. Fill one with compost in the usual way. In the other, insert the neck of a cola bottle prepared as above, but extended with a tube cut from plastic milk bottles and secured with industrial-strength adhesive tape.

You can now both topwater through the collar and feed the roots as the plant matures.

Don't worry about any gaps that remain between your bottle and the
soil. A few waterings will fill them in...

Compost

An infusion of well matured compost is said to contain
every nutrient a plant needs. This is not surprising, given
the *smorgasbord* of weeds and vegetable trimmings that
has gone into it.

Make it in the same way as manure tea.

Compost infusion can also be sprayed to deter fungal
infections and, whether used as a foliar or root feed, it
contains a wealth of beneficial microorganisms that
allegedly help plants resist pests and disease.

Seaweed

Seaweed is very rich in trace elements plus up to 13%
potash, much needed by leeks, celeriac, celery and fruiting
tomatoes and cucurbits.

It has an N-P-K ratio identical to fresh cow manure.

It is illegal in the UK to pick live seaweed and, at time of
writing, somebody was fined heavily for plucking sea lettuce
to feed his tortoise.

Methinks, he should also have been fined for cruelty to animals.

But *dead* seaweed is (or should be) another matter,
especially if retrieved from a private beach. Your local
council might even welcome you - a volunteer
conservationist - clearing that smelly detritus from their
tourist havens.

Stack it in the open for a few weeks, and turn it
occasionally, so rain can leach out the worst of the salt.

You'll never get it all out. Don't worry. A low concentration of salt,
added to fertile soil, actually makes the soil *more* fertile.

Then treat it like fresh comfrey and rot it down in a
Comfrey Tea Pot for three weeks, with just a little water.

The iodine in seaweed is said to lock up the magnesium in
the soil, rendering it unavailable to plants. A gentle
sprinkling of Epsom salts (*magnesium sulphate*) should
remedy that, especially if you use a *lot* of seaweed and plan
to grow tomatoes.

> Of course, Epsom salts are also said to lock up the calcium in the soil,
> making it less available to plants.
>
> (I *knew* we should never have got onto this topic...)

A word of caution

All the above infusions have an extra dimension - odour.

In fact, a month old tub of comfrey tea smells *exactly* like a
cow shed.

If you are misguided enough to slosh any of the infusions
above on your house plants, burn incense, boil some cloves
or open a pot of vinegar in the room.

The good news is, the smell will *probably* vanish - before your
spouse does.

Chapter 17

Composition of organic fertilisers

Nitrogen sources

	N%	P%	K%
Hoof and bone meal	14	2	0
Bat or bird guano	8-19	4-31	2
Blood meal	12.5	1.1	1
Feather meal	13.6	0.3	0.2
Crab-shell meal	8.2	1.5	0.5
Fish emulsion	4-5	2-4	1-2
Fish meal	10.5	6	0.5
Soybean meal	6	2	2
Cottonseed meal	3-6	2	1-2
Wheat bran	2.9	1.4	1.3
Alfalfa meal	2.5	0.3	1.9
Peat	1-3	0.5	1
Worm castings	1	0	0
Soot, from chimney	1-11	1	-
Coffee grounds, dried	2	-	1

Phosphorous sources

	N%	P%	K%
Bone meal (up to 30% calcium)	3	20	0
Rock phosphate (up to 30% calcium)	0	33	0
Oyster shell	-	10	-

Potash (potassium) sources

	N%	P%	K%
Greensand (22 trace minerals)	0	1.5	6-7
Granite dust (67% silica)	0	0	3-5
Kelp (33% trace minerals)	1	0	1.2

	N%	P%	K%
Wood ashes (raises soil pH)	0	1	1-10
Seaweed	1-2	0-1	5-13
Banana skins (ash)	-	3.25	42
Cucumber skins (ash) (also high phosphorous)	-	11.28	27
Citrus fruit peel (ash)	-	-	31
Potato skins, raw (ash)	-	5	27
Bean stems & pods (ash)	-	5	18

All three nutrients

	N%	P%	K%
Comfrey	2	3	5
Nettles	3	2	3
Compost	1-3	0.5-1	1-3
Manure, cow	0.25	0.15	0.25
Manure, horse	0.3	0.15	0.5
Manure, poultry	2-6	2-4	1-3
Sewage sludge	2-6	3-7	0-1

Some exotic sources

	N%	P%	K%
Harbour mud	1	1	-
N York City garbage	3-4	1	2-4
Dried jellyfish	4.6	-	-
King crab, dried	10	-	-
Lobster shells	5	4	-

Note: the above percentages are drawn from several authorities and each authority cites varying figures, based upon different samples. The sample might have been wet or dry, fresh, aged or burnt, etc, so the figures are unreliable.

For example, fresh seaweed has an N-P-K ratio similar to that of fresh cow manure, yet this is not apparent from the Table.

However, exact percentages are unimportant. What *is* useful to note is the ratio *between nutrients* in each source - and the gross comparisons between different *kinds* of organic fertiliser.

Chapter 18

Organic solutions to plant problems

A YeoPod is a little fortress, virtually immune to pests that creep, crawl, scratch or tunnel.

Yet sometimes YeoPods *can* be threatened by determined marauders like deer and flying insects.

Soil-borne diseases pose less of a risk than in conventional beds because the soil in each pod is (usually) replenished each season. That said, air-borne diseases like blight and the myriad variations of mildew are always with us.

The remedies that work for conventional beds work equally well for YeoPods. For example:

WARM-BLOODED PESTS

Birds

Birds rarely venture into the rim of a YeoPod, fearing a trap, and they are usually no problem with mature vegetables. But birds *can* devastate a row of new peas, or make confetti out of young leaves.

Hang foil crisp packets, inside out, from canes thrust into or beside the pods. *Or* CDs. *Or* tinsel.

Or plastic shopping bags. These work very well, in my experience. They toss and puff out in the wind, forever changing their shape - which confuses birds that soon learn to ignore a static scarecrow.

> If you *must* build a scarecrow to amuse the children, give it a long coat and erect it over a YeoPod. You can then blanch chicory or endive in the darkened YeoPod.

Netting may be the only answer with a serious invasion of

eg. ducks, pheasants or pigeons.

But YeoPods provide a convenient base to which a net bag can easily be attached.

This can be dropped over four canes, their tips protected by little plastic cola bottles or yogurt pots.

Make a bag from ¼ inch mesh and tack the edges of the mesh together with industrial-strength staples or twists of wire.

Cats

One member reported that her cats used the pods as scratching posts.

If this is a problem, remember that cats hate strong smells - curry, garam marsala, garlic and especially citrus.

A few lemon or grapefruit rinds scattered around should deter them.

Cat lovers will hate me for saying this but... if you don't mind being unkind, a bottle half full of ammonia - buried between the pods - will see them off for an entire season.

These remedies also work in conventional seedbeds. As do layers of twigs or holly leaves.

Children

Shame on you! Children are not a pest but a blessing. They should be *encouraged* to visit your YeoPods.

Pay them five pence for every weed they pull from the pods' peripheries (and deduct five pence for every irreplaceable plant they pull from the YeoPods by mistake), and you've infused in them forever the joy of gardening.

Plus... they'll very soon be able to repay your mortgage.

Deer

Even a tall fence is no deterent to a feisty Spring deer.

However, deer - like many animals - loathe the smell of sulphur. That's probably why sulphurous garlic is often advocated as a repellant. In US trials, deterrents based on sulphurous rotten eggs outperformed all others.

So periodically break an egg into each pod. Better still, smear rotten eggs on posts at your garden's entry points.

Failing that, feral cat dung - like tiger dung from your local zoo - deters almost *all* warm-blooded pests.

> Except Planning Officrs, of course. But these are not warm-blooded.

Put it in a sealed margarine tub, with holes in the side. You don't want such toxic excreta near your vegetables or in your soil.

Moles

Wire mesh laid across the base of the pods prevents moles from tunnelling up into the collars. However, there are very few humane remedies for moles that burrow *through* the cones.

Over the centuries, every manner of noisy device or odorous thing like camphor, paraffin, burning sulphur, creosote, jeyes fluid, old socks, and the like, has been stuffed into their holes - but only with mixed results.

Simply rejoice that, the more mole tunnels you acquire, *the more friable will be your ground...*

Rabbits

A mature rabbit might indeed be able to nibble leafy vegetables from a one foot pod. The remedies above for *deer* should work.

It's also said that raw liver juice, diluted in water, is a deterrent.

Or build your pods over old smelly dog blankets (obtainable from kennels), with holes cut above the cones so the roots can descend into them.

If rabbit tunnels are your problem, lay the pods over sheets of wire mesh that extend across the ground at least four feet in all directions.

Rats, mice and voles

Few rodents will have the savvy to burrow under a pod, then navigate upwards. If they do, the ultimate remedy is as for moles and rabbits - a fine wire mesh laid under the pod.

Rodents eat the fleshy parts of tubers, for the most part. As these grow in the pod, not the cone, your vegetables should be well protected.

However, a large rat or squirrel (a 'tree rat') might still reach the top of a pod and, in a hungry season, do some harm. Lay camphor (crushed mothballs) mixed with bran within the pod rim and this should deter or kill them.

It's also a very reliable remedy for slugs and snails, in the unlikely event that these surmount the pod walls.

> Molluscs won't readily climb over a band of grease mixed with soot or salt, brushed around the walls. Or a band of copper wire.

INSECTS

So many are the organic defences against insect invasions - compiled over centuries - that I tremble to list them all. Especially as few of them work anyway.

A few well-proven rules of thumb are:

If you find it on leaves...

spray it with an emulsion of garlic, oil and soapy water.

> The garlic is arguable, as 'tis the soap and oil that seals their breathing holes and kills them.

One recipe I've proven is: 1 tsp of liquid dishwashing soap shaken up with 4oz of chopped garlic and one cup of vegetable (or baby) oil in one quart of water. Leave for 48 hours. Strain. Then spray.

> Of course, lazy gardeners will simply slosh on their soapy bath water...

This *does* work with aphids, blackfly, caterpillars and most other bugs that feast on leaves, I find.

A large invasion of aphids, eg. on broad beans, can be removed in moments by rolling over them a wide piece of adhesive tape.

Caterpillars on mature plants can also be killed by spraying them briefly with water just a few degrees below boiling point. Amazingly, this rarely harms the plant.

> Or shake wood ash over them from the end of a nylon stocking.

If it flies...

deter or confuse it with strong odours.

Carrot fly can allegedly be deterred by spraying the carrot tops frequently with diluted essential oils of the kinds used in aromatherapy. Almost *any* smelly oil is said to work.

> More usually, a thick rampart of onions, garlic or chives is grown around the carrots for the same purpose, but this is not really practical with YeoPods.

Thrips, whitefly, fruit flies and other little insects that hop or flutter can be sucked up with a portable vacuum cleaner.

But dare you open the bag?

If it buries...

mask the soil with pieces of carpet, tinfoil or cardboard. This is very easy in a YeoPod.

Rhubarb stems thrust beside brassica were once a fabled deterrent to cabbage root fly, until trials found they didn't work. Likewise, chilli, curry powder and other strong substances scattered round the plant have arguable results.

Organic gardeners have - since Ayurvedic times - tried to repel insect pests with sprayed infusions of basil, rhubarb, elder, nettles, neem and many other leaves.

Like herbal medicine, these no doubt work magnificently at times... but so many are the variables in any garden, and between any season, that definitive conclusions have never - to my knowledge - been published.

> Of these, only Neem - an Asian shade-tree - comes with a well-attested pedigree as a pest deterrent. But, I can reliably attest, having once grown it, Neem seed is *unheard of* in the UK.

DISEASES

If you took the textbooks seriously, you would never grow anything - because their thickest chapters are usually devoted to 'Garden Troubles'...

So many are the diseases they list that I will not dare to offer remedies for them all - especially as so often the only reliable organic answer is "*Burn the affected plant at once*".

Yet serious diseases rarely occur if good garden hygiene is practised and many so-called 'diseases' are nothing of the sort anyway.

Just mirages

For example, if your young legume leaves are yellow this may be *nitrogen chlorosis*, caused by nitrogen deficiency in the soil. It's harmless and usually corrects itself as the plant grows.

Many years ago, I was once delighted to see my tomato plants develop attractive purple leaves. Was this a new variety of tomato, I asked, worthy of immortalising in my seed bank?

> No, it was simply *phosphorous deficiency*, brought about because I had been too lazy to renew the soil in a GrowBag.

Tomato leaves are also notorious for rolling up as if some noxious insect is nesting within. But it's usually only *Summer Leaf Curl*, probably the plant's way of limiting water loss. It doesn't harm the plant.

When my young nasturtium leaves became cream and parchment-like in the greenhouse, I suspected some exotic disorder - till I realised they were merely *sunburnt*.

If your leaf edges suddenly wrinkle and die, it may be just *wind damage* - or a snap frost - rather than disease.

> If the bad weather persists, shroud the plant in a clear perforated plastic bag. Even a collar cut from a big cardboard box will keep out wind and mild frost.

YeoPods resist disease

Disease is far less likely to affect a plant grown in a YeoPod than in the naked soil.

Why? Because the environment is much more closely controlled.

That said, if you see even a hint of disease, you will be wise to take up the collars and canes at season's end and scrub and soak them in a solution of bleach or Jeyes solution

The classic organic (indeed, biodynamic) remedies for disease seek to stimulate the plant's *immune system* to resist the infestation, rather than to repel the invaders themselves.

So to combat blight in tomatoes and potatoes, or mould on cucurbits, we see frequent admonitions to spray infusions of marestail, comfrey, nettles, compost, manure, milk, garlic, chives, rhubarb, elder or aromatic herbs.

The observant reader will note that these are curiously similar to many of the organic remedies also prescribed for insect pests.

In both cases, we are urged to spray the infusions at the first sign of a problem, so they will fortify the plant to resist it.

Disease and pests prey on weakness

Organic doctrine says a healthy plant does not easily get disease - or attract pests. These problems occur largely with *un*healthy plants.

They are Nature's way of culling the weaklings so only the most robust plants will survive to set seed.

Certainly, the great garden predators like molluscs, wood lice and millipedes seem to favour the weakest plants.

So when you apply an organic remedy against disease or insects, you are *not* wickedly using unregulated medications or pesticides - but benignly strengthening the plants' *inner vitality!*

This distinction is important as...

in the UK, it is now illegal under the tyranny of EC laws to use any organic formulations as herbicides, pesticides or disease-repellants that are not on its approved list.

Its 'approved' formulations include chemicals which can kill you. They *exclude* all the organic ideas above, most of which - if applied sensibly - can not harm you at all.

However, should you ever suffer a dawn raid from DEFRA inspectors, alerted to your illegal habit of spraying your bath water on your brassica, simply protest that you are applying a 'foliar feed'. It will enhance the plants' immune systems!

I'm told - with what truth, I know not - that the bureaucrats have no legitimate answer to that. They will slink away, *their handcuffs dragging in the dust...*

Chapter 19

How to predict your own climate

'Candlemas Day stick beans in the clay.'

For serious gardeners, to predict the climate in their garden - and far more accurately than any regional newspaper or television forecast - is an absolute necessity.

But even with modern technology, *it doesn't get easier.*

Climatic change has cast doubt on the old 'planting date' truisms - and these were themselves never more than fable.

The admonition above - to set out beans on 2nd February - still makes sense in the UK for broad beans (favas) which are remarkably hardy, or for round peas under cloches.

But it will *not* serve for climbing beans. Indeed, it will not serve at all if your soil is soggy or frozen.

The naked truth

Time was, gardeners were advised to sow their seeds naked - the gardeners, that is.

This is admirable advice. If you can't sow seed outdoors naked without suffering hypothermia, your soil is too chilly.

More sophisticated attempts at geomancy, at least in the garden, have included the global assignment of geographic 'zones' to predict growing conditions. But these are absurd. They make no allowance for the extreme weather variations possible even within one small post or zipcode district.

> For example, the US zone system puts me (in central UK) in zone 8 - similar to southern France and northern Spain. So I should be able to grow aubergines (egg plants), crowder peas and sweet potatoes outdoors.

But I *can't*.

The north west tip of Scotland, where pineapples grow outdoors in favoured coves warmed by the Gulf Stream, is given the same zone as the chilly heart of Sweden.

Where pineapples do *not* grow outdoors...

As a lazy man, I prefer the Ivinghoe Aston system of weather forecasting:

"if I can see Ivinghoe Beacon, it's going to rain; if I can't see Ivinghoe Beacon, it *is* raining. In either case, *I shouldn't be gardening...*"

Accept no substitutes

There is no substitute for keeping your own weather records over many years, specific to the micro-climate of *your* own garden.

Only then will you know *when* to sow each crop, and *where* each crop does best, according to your local temperatures, light, moisture and wind.

These factors may be entirely different from your neighbour's and can vary enormously even within a small garden.

And the more complicated your garden design is... the *more* they will vary.

Remarkable protection

YeoPods are flexible enough to give remarkable protection against weather extremes.

But *when* you set out the plants, and *where* you site the pods, can still make a crucial difference between good crops - and bounteous ones.

No weather factors are predictable in a garden, apart from frost dates, 'heat units' and light patterns - and even these are not inviolable guides.

Wind, temperature, humidity and precipitation can *not* be forecast - at least, in any detail useful for gardeners - for more than a day or two.

Such forecasts may be fine for tactical gardening. "Is it worth going to the allotment tomorrow - or not?".

But they're useless for strategic planning. "Shall I germinate my tomatoes this week - *or wait a month?*".

> One Guild member in the Shetlands said that one year she was still cropping outdoor tomatoes in late October. Next year, she couldn't even see the garden that month - for horizontal hail.

> Neither of these months bore any relation to the climatic 'averages' for her area.

Frost dates

If you grow any frost-sensitive plant outdoors, you *must* establish the first and last frost date for your immediate area.

I'm told that US readers can often find these dates, and much other weather data, from a host of government agencies or even from local airports, radio or newspaper stations.

> UK and other European readers may not be so fortunate.

Your best advice will come from neighbourhood gardeners or allotment owners or the secretaries of local gardening or farming societies.

> My neighbouring 'pick your own' farm is a fount of wisdom, I find. Likewise my rural pub.

But the dates must be local.

One Internet weather site vaguely gives for my nearest town, just eight miles from me, a last frost date of 'early May' and a first frost date of 'October'.

Yet it's wrong. From pained experience I *know* I dare not set out beans, peppers or tomatoes without cloches before 1st June - and I'd better get them all in before 20th October, latest. When the killer frosts hit.

Those dates have never failed me.

> Even then, one year I had two mild - but fortunately not lethal - frosts as early as mid-September.

> With frost dates, it's wise to build in a *large* margin for error!

Once you know your frost dates, you can also extend your growing season at each end with a judicious use of cloches.

YeoPods make this easy.

But few things in a garden are more disheartening than to rear a row of precious plants under cloches then blithely whip off the cloches, *just one day before the last killer frost...*

Another great benefiit of knowing the first frost date peculiar to your own garden is... you can calculate *backwards* from that date to know when to set out frost-tolerant plants beforehand.

> For example, onion sets might go in 16 weeks before the last frost date and Brussels sprouts eight weeks before. So in my garden, I know it's safe to plant onions in early February and Brussel sprouts in early April.

> Your dates will be different!

A guide to planting dates for every popular vegetable - as ruled by the last frost date - is given in Chapter 21. But please note, it can be no more than a crude guide.

To know if a snap frost is threatened...

investigate the weather sites on the Internet.

You just *can't* rely on regional newspapers, radio or television.

I won't recommend any specific web addresses because these - and their quality and contents - change by the hour.

However, web weather sites *can* be invaluable.

I was most impressed...

by one site that forecast the weather in my own postcode area ten days ahead, and predicted a ground frost - in my paddock, to the very night, *five days ahead...*

Other sites which I have also found amazingly accurate give early warnings of potato and tomato blight.

To find these sites, input '"weather" or "blight" - or whatever - into your favourite search engine, *plus* any geographical filters you wish - like 'uk', or your county or postcode area. And see what joys emerge.

'Heat units'

Heat units are quite different from average monthly temperatures.

The latter can vary widely, year on year, and it's no consolation to know that your 'average' temperature for April is 58°F - if your soil is still frost-hard.

Instead, heat units measure the *total amount of warmth* that your garden receives during the growing season. By keeping records for several years, you can predict - with astonishing accuracy - how many days you need to harvest any given crop.

So if a catalogue promises vaguely '70 days' for a certain tomato variety, you can refer instead to your heat units record and discover that - in your garden - it needs precisely eg. 998 heat units.

You can then forecast during the season *almost the exact day* the first fruits of that tomato variety will ripen.

You can then plan your succession planting accordingly, and start germinating the next batch of plants.

Heat units are the way that commercial growers predict the time to roll out their harvesting machines. *It works...*

To record the heat units for your garden...

and for every crop, calculate the *average temperature* in the garden on the day you set out the crop.

That means, take the highest temperature recorded during daylight hours and the lowest, and divide by two.

Then subtract from this the *'base temperature'.*

This is an arbitrary number, chosen simply for reference purposes, but it *must* remain consistent in all your subsequent recordings.

For example, for temperate plants like brassica you might assign a base temperature of **40°F** and for exotic (warm climate) crops like tomatoes and climbing beans, assign **55°F**.

So... suppose you set out a trellis of Cherokee Trail of Tears beans in YeoPods on 1st June, and the average temperature that day was 57°F.

Subtract the base temperature for warm climate crops (55°F) and your heat units for that day are 2.

(On some cool days, the heat units may indeed be negative values.)

From your records over the years, you may then find that Cherokee Trail of Tears beans - if 'station sown' outdoors in the bare soil - need 55 heat units to germinate, 930 heat units to be fit for table use and 1440 before they dry on the vine for seed harvesting.

However, your ultra-early Tiger bean may need only 690 heat units before it's ready to crop for supper and 910 heat units before the pods are dry enough to store.

Each variety will have its own different total of heat units, apt just to *your* garden.

You can make precise predictions

By recording how these heat units accumulate over the season, you can predict - fairly accurately - when a crop is ready to take out of the ground.

And perhaps defer your holiday that week?

You can also have modules of eg. Spring cabbages ready to replace the beans, at exactly the right time.

How will you know just *when* the brassica (etc) is ready to set out? *Look at their heat units!*

For this insight, I am indebted to *The Big Book of Gardening Secrets*, Charles W G Smith, Storey Publishing.

Light patterns

One issue in which all textbooks concur is that, if you grow tall plants in rows or trellises, the rows should be aligned **North-South** so each plant gets the maximum light.

I once scoffed at this advice.

Commonsense told me that, if plants are aligned North-

South, the shadows on them would be deep and continuous - first on their Western side as the sun rose in the East and then their other side as it set in the West.

However, if the rows are aligned West-East, the sun would not cast long side shadows and the foliage would gain maximum light. Or so I reasoned.

Several Guild members hastened to correct me.

'The quality of the sun at sunrise and sunset is nowhere near as good as the sun at full high noon, and trellises set North to South get the best high noon sunlight,' one said.

'The sun does *not* rise in the East and set in the West!' another pointed out.

'In the northern hemisphere, it describes an *arc* - moving from South East to South West.

So with a north-south orientation, all the trellises get an equal amount of sun - with the majority of the equal sunlight falling during midday (roughly 10am to 4pm) when it does the most good.

'Orient them east/west and the most southerly trellises get a lot of sun but throw their shadow on the northerly ones.'

Yet another member added:

'With a north-south orientation, not only do the trellises get the maximum sun but also the crops growing on either side of the trellises. With an east-west orientation, it would be difficult to grow much to the North of the trellis at all in a normal dull UK summer.

'The plants would be in perpetual shade.'

Sceptical, I rushed into the garden where I had scrupulously aligned my YeoPod trellises east-west.

Yay, the heaviest growth of beans on every trellis was *indeed* on the South West sides. As my members had predicted.

So I concede, sometimes the textbooks are right...

But I consoled myself by noting I had done at least *one* thing well. Our predominate Summer winds blow from East to West. In July, we have been known to get hurricanes.

I might have mentioned this...

By aligning the trellises east-west, I had - like a skilful yachtsman in a gale, albeit accidentally - *set their smallest profile to the wind.*

So this year no trellis had blown over. Whereas in the prior year, Force 8 winds had tossed my trellises from Luton to Birmingham.

Sometimes in a garden, you have to make trade offs.

But if hurricanes are *not* your problem, do align your YeoPod trellises - or any rows of large plants within YeoPods - **North-South**. Provided you are at liberty to do this.

If you can't, console yourself. *All gardeners* have to make trade offs...

Light is a Good Thing

Light in a garden is one of the four main components of healthy plant growth, along with good soil, warmth and water. So it's well worth checking how much shade your garden gets, and where.

And it's not always obvious.

On a sunny midSummer day, take photos of your garden from all directions. In a simple rectangular plot, you may need just four elevations - facing north, south, east and west.

In a complicated garden having many alcoves and walls, you'll need to take a *lot* of photos!

Take one set in early morning, one set at high noon and one set in late noon.

Nooks are a Bad Thing

At once, you will understand why your strawberry basket is *not* doing well in its picturesque Nook. For ten hours out of 14 in high Summer, it's bathed in shade!

You will also discover the sunniest spots that luxuriate in light all day.

So why waste swiss chard, kale, beetroot, landcress, spinach, carrots, peas, brassica, tubers, rhubarb or lettuce there? They can cope with mild or intermittent shade.

Answer: transfer them - the decorative rainbow chard, at least - to the Nook.

Instead, set out tomatoes, squash, sweet corn, sweet peppers and other 'fruiting' plants in those favoured sun-rich spots.

You will realise at last why to plant loganberries along your North-facing fence in front of tall trees was an error.

I repeat merely my own mistake of some years back.

They're perpetually in shade!

You'll move them at once (as I did) to the South-facing fence, and replace them with comfrey, Good King Henry and jerusalem artichokes which grow almost anywhere.

If you can bear the labour of it...

take photos *again* around both the Spring Equinox (22nd March) and Autumn Equinox (22nd September).

The elevation of the sun, and the shadows it throws, are

quite different at these times.

Such photos will give you valuable guidance on where best to extend the season at either end by using cloched YeoPods.

Consigning a cloched plant to a region of permanent shade is futile. Deep frost apart, most temperate plants can cope with chilly weather. But in low-light days, they need all the *sun* they can get!

You'll also find that areas of continual shade are usually frost pockets. Yet another reason to keep cloched plants out of them...

Shade is not always bad.

In hot climates, you'll *want* to keep your peas, lettuce and other leafy plants in partial shade or... either they won't grow anyway, or you'll be forever watering them.

> For this reason, a member in the Mediterranean grows them under short tube cloches of *black* plastic, open both ends so only slanting light reaches the crops, and only for a very few hours.

> A cloche of wickerwork or white muslin will also shield leafy plants in sustained bright sun.

Sweet peppers are said to crop better in the partial shade of sunflowers or sweet corn. Peas *(Pisa sativum)* positively enjoy the low light and foggy weather of a British Spring, and perish or develop powdery mildew in a hot dry season.

Conversely, crowder (field) peas - of the same *Vigna* family as mung and adzuki - will crop *only* in a long, dry, bright and hot season.

Young transplants should also be shielded from long periods of direct sunlight.

Fortunately, the YeoPod design makes it easy to rig

cardboard shades on the pods' south-facing sides so the plants get only a few hours sunlight at noon.

When light is poor, crumpled tinfoil can be thrust into the top of the pod to throw all available light back up to the leaves. This *does* make a big difference.

It also impedes evaporation.

Tip: try putting big stones or tiles wrapped in tinfoil around strawberries you grow in the open soil and you'll see how much quicker they ripen.

Only *do* check periodically for slugs lurking under the tiles...

One member even wired upturned *lampshades* lined with tinfoil over his pods, when planting brassica in Spring. They had the added benefit of catching rain.

Rain

It's very easy to deliver water to YeoPods without waste, using a hose or watering can, and then to mulch the tops so evaporation is minimal.

These factors are important in a drought or where a hosepipe ban compels us to use watering cans filled from a butt.

Rainwater is always better than tapwater because...

it contains no chlorine, flouride or lime and, collected in a butt, will be at ambient temperature - the same as the plant.

However, there is little truth in the adage that we should water transplants *only* with ambient-temperature water, lest we chill them.

Chilly tapwater, if we must use it, does little harm - even to young plants. *Or so I read.*

Indeed, spray tomatoes and other bushy plants with cool water at 41°-59°F - ie. *much* lower than ambient temperature - and it's a good thing. You'll have bushier plants because it gives them a mild shock. *Or so I read.*

> But surely (I wondered) tomatoes sprayed with cool water might go on to develop Blossom End Rot - which is one proven reaction to shock?

> *On this important dilemma, the jury is still out...*

Moral: never believe one word you hear or read from gardening experts. (Except here, of course...)

What *is* certain is that the *degree* of water available to the plant will dictate week on week - all other factors apart - its **growth.**

Heed the Wisdom of the Water Guru

Commercial growers know *precisely* how to get their plants to the right stage for garden centre sales during the UK's Easter holiday buying peak. They control the water.

> "If the plant's racing ahead, I withhold water," one water guru told me. "If it's slow, I increase water. But you have to know exactly how *much* to water in each case, and *when.*"

> So complex and important is this skill that the Water Guru is often the company's highest paid employee.

Make your own Rain Gauge

You can easily tell how much rainwater falls on your garden... using no more than an open jamjar and a ruler.

Place it in an unobstructed place, the ruler within.

Every half-inch of rainwater in the jar means around two gallons of rain have fallen per square yard (or metre, if you prefer).

This is a good test of a rotating garden sprinkler, the kind that throws water intermittently across a wide arc.

Place the jamjars at various points among your plants.

You'll discover such a sprinkler must be in action for several hours to give the plants any useful volume of water whatsoever - and 90% of it is utterly wasted.

What's a useful volume?

One watering should deliver the equivalent of one inch of rain or four gallons per square yard.

Much more than this will be needed in hot weather because as much as ½ gallon per day will be evaporated before the plants can even take it up.

How to water a YeoPod

Such figures apply to conventional gardening in open soil.

YeoPods are different.

For a YeoPod that's nine inches at the base, and well mulched, provide as much as *four pints* of water a week. Smaller or larger pods, cool or hot weather, moderate or inebriate plants will dictate less or more water.

A big mature indeterminate tomato plant like Big Boy may need as much as *four gallons* of water per day, in very hot weather. A truly giant squash like a marrow or pumpkin might need up to eight gallons.

It's easy to prove how thirsty squash plants are for water.

In hot weather, simply set an open dish of water beside a dehydrated squash plant. Within 48 hours, its tendrils will have visibly *crept* several inches across the soil - toward the water.

Plants in a mulched YeoPod may do well enough for two weeks without watering - for example, if you're away on holiday - but regular watering brings the fastest growth.

In hot weather particularly, it's important to get water *down* to the GrowCone. A few cupfuls won't do it.

You can't overdo it

Fortunately, it is very difficult indeed to overwater a YeoPod - provided the GrowCone wasn't rammed into ceramic-hard clay.

Why? The collar leaks away any surplus top water and the cone, while retaining moisture, slowly drains away the excess.

After watering, of course, be sure the top mulch is intact.

The **Forefinger Test** is an easy way to tell if a pod needs watering. Thrust your forefinger in down to the knuckle and, if the soil at your fingertip is dry, the pod needs watering.

Do this too often, of course, and you'll have no further gardening worries because the plants will all be dead - their roots scrambled by your questing finger.

So we must use Keyhole Surgery.

Insert a stubby piece of cane in the soil in the collar when setting out the transplant. The roots will grow around it.

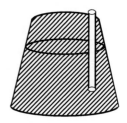

When a moisture test is required, remove

the cane gently with a screwing motion and you can insert your finger, test the soil and replace the cane without overly disturbing the roots.

An even lazier option...

is to water *only* when the plants are wilting.

But if you rush to over-water a wilting tomato plant when it's in fruit, the fruit may burst.

> 'Feast and famine' watering for a sweet pepper may bring on Blossom End Rot.

> Climbing beans get confused by panic watering, amid long dry spells, and may not set flowers or pods.

> And salad plants need *continual* lavish watering lest they bolt or become tough.

Better is to establish a regular watering routine and keep a close check on soil moisture during protracted hot weather.

> **A tip:** the wider your hose, the more water it delivers per hour. At 40psi, a ½" hose gives 523 gallons per hour, a 5/8" hose 959 gallons per hour, and a ¾" hose 1570 gallons per hour.

> So a ¾" commercial-size hose will let you water your garden in *one third* the time as a skimpy ½" hose - the coiled kind sold by garden centres with 57 dinky plastic fittings.

> These are guaranteed to have a nervous breakdown at the first sight of a faucet.

> Not many people know this...

Wind

If your garden is in a specially windy or exposed spot, YeoPods are a blessing.

While they *do* raise the plant above ground, they also give superb anchorage and root protection.

So... if you grow tall plants like sweet corn, indeterminate tomatoes, brussel sprouts and the like, simply sink the rootball *on top* of the GrowCone, ie. at soil level, and *earth it up* within the collar as the plant grows.

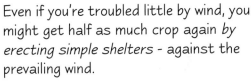

In areas subject to gales, you may have to be content to grow dwarf varieties.

Indeed, if you grow them to maturity within a very large collar - with a perforated plastic film over the top, they will be protected from the elements from cradle to grave in their own little cold frames.

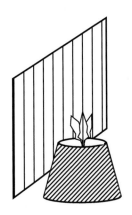

Even if you're troubled little by wind, you might get half as much crop again *by erecting simple shelters* - against the prevailing wind.

Low horizontal strips of hessian (burlap) or willow hurdles erected in front of vulnerable plants like lettuce are effective.

Windbreaks do not just shield plants from physical buffeting but also mitigate the effects of wind chill and frost. But they *must* be permeable.

Solid walls can be worse than useless. The wind just leaps over them and twists into destructive eddies on the other side.

One simple windbreak...

is a triple row of sunflowers or Jerusalem artichokes. These are so robust they can be sown - in friable soil, at least - in a GrowCone *without* a collar.

A block of sweetcorn is another idea.

If all else fails, sow a thick bank of *nettles* between your plants and the wind.

Don't laugh. You'll have a self-perpetuating windbreak that stays effective throughout Winter and grows lush again in good time to repel the Spring gales.

> Nettles can easily be propagated from roots or stem cuttings, and they are *not* (unacceptably) invasive.

Your nettlebank will then not only be delightful to butterflies but will also keep marauders out of your allotment.

When it's no longer needed, you can turn it into nettle tea - *or eat it.*

Create your own old wive's tales

If you would like to rediscover the wisdom of those old gardeners, but updated to modern times, I commend you to

Phenology:

> 'the study of recurring phenomena as influenced by climactic conditions'.

Nature doesn't read gardening calendars.

That's why the calendars published in gardening magazines are - like horoscopes - better used for recreation than instruction.

> I especially love their titles: 'Work to do this month'. If it's 'work', you *shouldn't be doing it, anyway!*

In a garden, phenology is the art of learning *from Nature* - what to do and when to do it.

Simple phenology

For example, if you see daffodils blooming it's time to plant onions, spinach, Swiss chard, spinach, salsify, peas and leeks. This date may or may not be precisely 12 weeks before your last frost date but, when in doubt, prefer *Nature's advice* to the calendar's.

> When my Mercury (Good King Henry) dies back in Autumn - and my collards grow tough, I know it's time to sink hard-necked garlic.

> When my crocuses and snowdrops bloom in early Spring, and the first pink sporulating stems of marestail thrust skyward in my paddock, I plant broad beans.

> When my apple and cherry trees shed their first blossoms in early Summer, I sow french beans.

> When my wife's peonies flower in mid-Summer, I set out late tomatoes and squash.

And so forth.

So simple!

Keep a detailed diary of such indicators as they occur in *your* garden - what first flowers when, the first flight of martins, the first fruit formation, the first leaf falls, the first bean to set flowers - and the first fresh pods to occur, and the like.

You can then cross-relate those occurences to *other* data like heat units, frost dates and even pest patterns.

In time, you will have a unique logbook that will enable you to plot the optimum sowing and harvesting times for every plant.

In *your* garden.

You may then be able to say with impressive confidence:

'At Candlemas, I'll mow the grass!'

And nobody will be able to confute you.

Chapter 20

Questions frequently asked about YeoPods

Q. I'm about to go on holiday for two weeks.

Should I purchase an automatic watering system so that every YeoPod is watered regularly in my absence?

A. To set up an automatic system, with a little computer to regulate the frequency of watering, will set you back at least £50 at time of writing.

If you have a *lot* of YeoPods, your cost will be as long as a piece of string or - to be precise - the equivalent length in watering tube.

To put this in perspective - and to educate my great grand children who will (I hope) centuries from now hunt this book down at computerised book sites - you could as of this date buy for that hard-earned £50, while on holiday, *20 litres of fizzy lager.*

Or... 15 bottles of an undrinkable Chablis or 18 Big Mac hamburgers with small fries.

Far fewer on the French Riviera, of course, but more in Florida.

Yes, a watering system is a much wiser investment.

But there's no need for such anguished choices!

Simply water each YeoPod very intensively *before* you go. Saturate it, so the entire lower GrowCone also becomes wet. Then mulch the top of the collar with a thick cardboard disk, plastic shopping bag or a bunched up face towel.

You know you'd lose it on holiday, anyway.

Enough moisture should remain in the YeoPod to keep your plants alive for up to 14 days, even in hot weather.

Q: I don't have the patience to make up all those organic potting mixes for the GrowCone and the collar. Can't I just use topsoil in both, and water it with Miracle-Gro?

A: Yes, of course you can. You could also eat hamburgers and potato chips all day, washed down with diet coke!

You would survive for a while, after a fashion. So would your plants, fed in similar ways.

But they would grow like children fattened on junk food - obese, unhealthy and deficient in nutrients.

Chemical feeds do *nothing* for the soil, your posterity or your bank account. You have to keep buying them. This simply profits chemicals firms who have the morals of a mollusc. Like tobacco and GM-food manufacturers, they want to hook the world on their products.

Ethics apart, to fill a YeoPod with home-made (or cheaply acquired) organic ingredients is to be unashamedly *selfish*.

Organic gardening is selfish

Have you ever considered that organic gardening is *selfish*? It truly is.

Because...

> Such ingredients slowly improve the soil so that, one day, you may need little more or none of them.

> Your bank account (if not your bank manager) will bless you.

> You might also then bequeath to your children a true asset - pure humus-rich loam that, with only infrequent

refreshment, will forever grow them anything.

And most organic ingredients are *waste* products.

For a little barter or ingenuity, you might get all you need, free. You can *save* - over the lifetime of your garden - untold thousands of pounds. Which you might otherwise have spent on soil amendments and fertilisers.

Just think...

Think how many pints of Adnams beer even a saving of £1000 might procure?

> I concede, you might inexplicably have other priorities, like paying for the mortgage, your children's education, and your old age. Chemical fertilisers will help you with none of these, either...

That said, I see nothing wrong with using a *smidgen* of chemical fertiliser - if nothing else is to hand - to coax much-needed crops from utterly sterile soil. The first season, at least.

Or to kickstart a compost heap (ditto).

To do it again in the second season, however, is unforgiveable.

Oh, I nearly forgot... vegetables grown by organic means taste better (a fact disputed only by folk with vulcanised palates). Such vegetables have fewer toxins (indisputable). And they contain far more healthful vitamins and nutrients (ditto).

'Found lying in a road...'

Our first sight of the paddock

A hurricane in July

Ivinghoe Beacon in Summer

Marestail (Equisetum arvense)

The Challenge Ahead...

The Sunflower Forest takes shape

Ten foot sunflowers grown in GrowCones

The view from Mr Yeoman's deckchair

Onions thrive in GrowCones

A patio YeoPod

220 YeoPods adorn the paddock

Tomatoes rampant in YeoPods in late July

YeoPods when first set out

*YeoPods with tomato
transplants*

*The plants finds width -
and depth - in YeoPods*

If the soil is totally *impossible, set
collars on top of home-made GrowBags*

Squash transplants

Pumpkins love YeoPods

A glut of Patty Pans

Pumpkin flowers are edible

The fruit of the YeoPod

Chapter 21

The Plants Cornucopia

This is the most definitive guide to date to growing all the most popular edible plants - at least, those which grow in temperate climes - in YeoPods.

You may wonder why I have omitted Cucumbers. That is a good question.

Answer: My computer does not like Cucumbers. It bluntly refused to accept any text here referring to Cucumbers. So, fearing a mutiny (eg. 'Irrecoverable Error - *Refer to Manual*', followed by the Blue Screen of Death), I let it have its way...

No problem: simply treat your Cucumbers in all respects like Sweet Peppers (to which they bear no relationship whatsoever, of course) and they will fructify magnificently.

It is very important that you understand my cryptic references in these tables. So here is a helpful **Key** which should make every reference clear.

KEY to the Plants Cornucopia

CONVENTIONAL SPACING: Closer spacing is often possible in intensive beds (eg. no rows), or with catch cropping or using small cultivars.

SOIL CONDITION: using conventional methods. Also see ROTATION

SEEDLIFE: For ave. 50% germination if stored in cool, dry, dark conditions eg. in a sealed jar at no more than 50°F.

ISOLATION: The distances used by commercial growers to ensure seed purity and minimise cross-pollination from related species in the absence of caging. Lesser distances may be possible according to location and variety.

ROTATION: This model is based on a conventional 4-year rotation, which minimises disease and pest buildup and also produces successively, season after season, the types of soil each plant needs.

> **A** = Prefer very rich soil, even freshly manured.
> **B** = Require rich, well drained soil, ideally limed.
> **C** = Heavy feeders, requiring ample nitrogen.
> **D** = Light feeders, no recent lime or manure.
> **DX** = Odd plants & perennials, best grown in a dedicated plot.

PLANT OUT DATE: Specifies number of weeks before (or after) the last frost date when a plant may be safely sown or set out, outdoors. '0' is the last frost date eg. around 1st June in central UK. So '-12' means plant out 12 weeks *before* your last frost date. And '+4' means set out four weeks *after* your last frost date. Earlier planting is often possible under cloches or fleece.

Asparagus

'Asparagus officinalis' from family 'Liliaceae'

Habit: Perennial **Aspect:** Full sun to partial shade

Description: A plant of the lily family having small scaly or needle-like leaves and small red berries, of which the young shoots are cooked and eaten.

History: Derives from coastal areas of Europe and southern Russia. Known to the Romans and Gauls.

Notes: Plant one year-old crowns. Begin cutting spears only in year 3. Stop cutting in early Summer to let crowns develop for next year. A plant can be productive for up to 20 years.

GROWING GUIDE

Soil condition (conventional): Any rich soil, ideally sandy, but must be well drained

YeoPod mix (collar): JY5

YeoPod mix (cone): JY3A

Propagation: Can be grown from seed (in which case, spears should not be cut for three years) but usually from crowns, divided in winter, sunk in trenches 8in deep and 12 inches wide.

Conventional spacing (inches): 18/18 (rows/in rows)

Spacing in YeoPod: 1 crown per large collar

Days to pick: 750

Soil pH: 6.75-7.5

Plant yield: 20-25 spears

Water: Average watering. Mulch collar from early Spring with one inch of sand to suppress weeds.

Seed life: 5 years

Ideal Germination Temperature: 75°F

Isolation: 3200 yards

Optimum Growing Temperature: 60-85°F

Plant out date (weeks): -6

Seed germination: 15 days

Rotation: DX

Intercrop: n/a

Precede: Lettuce, Radishes, Spring Onions

To follow: Winter Lettuce, when ferns have died back

Comment: Asparagus demands the largest YeoPod possible, which should stay permanently in place.

Aubergine

Also known as Eggplant 'Solanum melongena' from family 'Solanaceae'

Habit: Annual **Aspect:** Sunny

Description: A tropical plant cultivated for its egg or truncheon-shaped shiny fruit, commonly dark purple but also white.

History: Derives from India and Burma. Grown in China in the 5th century BC, introduced to Europe by Arab traders in the 7th century.

Notes: Aubergines are perennials in the tropics. Grow like a sweet pepper, ie. in ample warmth, and preferably under glass in temperate zones.

GROWING GUIDE

Soil condition (conventional): Well drained, fertile and rich, sheltered, sunny location.

YeoPod mix (collar): JY5

YeoPod mix (cone): JY3A

Propagation: Sow in modules indoors, set out under cloches

Conventional spacing (inches): 24/24 (rows/in rows)

Spacing in YeoPod: one plant

Days to pick: 140

Soil pH: 6.0

Plant yield: 4-5lb

Water: Copious, when fruiting

Seed life: 7 years

Ideal Germination Temperature: 85°F

Isolation: 20 yards

Optimum Growing Temperature: 70-85°F

Plant out date (weeks): 0

Seed germination: 14-21 days

Rotation: DX

Intercrop: n/a

Precede: Carrots, Garlic, Parsley

To follow: Lettuce

Comment: Best grown in temperate climes in a greenhouse or polytunnel. If this has a solid base, use a collar of JY5 set on a GrowBag containing JY3A.

Beans, broad

Also known as Fava Beans *'Vicia faba'* from family *'Leguminosae'*

Habit: Annual *Aspect:* Full sun to partial shade

Description: An erect annual Eurasian bean plant, standard cultivars growing to four feet, cultivated for its large edible flattened seeds.

History: Grown from Bronze Age times in Europe. Found in Troy, Egyptian tombs and among bronze age artifacts. Grown in China from the 1st century AD and in the Sahara in the first millennium.

Notes: Broad beans are very hardy and can be sown in Autumn. But best yield is gained by an early-Spring sowing. Tall varieties will need supporting eg. with a cage.

GROWING GUIDE

Soil condition (conventional): Any rich, deep, manured, well drained soil, neutral to slightly acidic.

YeoPod mix (collar): JY5

YeoPod mix (cone): JY5

Propagation: From seed, planted outdoors in early Spring or (not advised) in Autumn

Conventional spacing (inches): 24/8

(rows/in rows)

Spacing in YeoPod: one plant

Days to pick: 98 (Spring)

Soil pH: 6.0-6.75

Plant yield: up to 2lb, shelled

Water: Ample, when fruiting

Seed life: 6 years

Ideal Germination Temperature: 75°F

Isolation: 1600 yards

Optimum Growing Temperature: 60-65°F

Plant out date (weeks): -12

Seed germination: 7-14 days

Rotation: B

Intercrop: Lettuce

Precede: nothing. Broad beans go in early.

To follow: Broccoli, Brussels sprouts, Cabbages, Cauliflowers, Collards, Kale, Kohlrabi

Beans, French

Also known as Haricot, Navy, Snap, Flageolet Beans *'Phaseolus vulgaris'* from family *'Leguminosae'*

Habit: Annual **Aspect:** Full sun to partial shade

Description: Beans yielding edible pods and seeds, eaten fresh in their entirety, or shelled, or dried for eg. soup. Dwarf cultivars grow to 18 inches, climbers to eight foot.

History: From South America, spread to western North America around 300BC. Climbing forms were brought to Europe in 16th century but the bush varieties were not cultivated in Europe until 18th century.

Notes: French beans are perennials in tropic climes.

GROWING GUIDE

Soil condition (conventional): Any rich, light, well drained soil

YeoPod mix (collar): JY1

YeoPod mix (cone): JY5

Propagation: From seed, sown in modules or degradeable pots and set out after last frost date. Can also be 'station sown' in collars outdoors after last frost date.

Conventional spacing (inches): 18/4 (rows/in rows)

Spacing in YeoPod: Climbing beans - 3 to 4 plants, subject to collar width. Dwarf beans - 1 to 2 plants, ditto.

Days to pick: 56-84

Soil pH: 6.0-7.5

Plant yield: up to 2lb fresh (climbers)

Water: Ample and constant, as soon as pods set

Seed life: 4 years

Ideal Germination Temperature: 80°F

Isolation: 3 yards

Optimum Growing Temperature: 60-70°F

Plant out date (weeks): 0

Seed germination: 7-14 days

Rotation: B

Intercrop: Climbing nasturtiums

Precede: Peas, Radishes

To follow: Broccoli, Brussels sprouts, Cabbages, Cauliflowers, Collards, Kale, Kohlrabi

Comment: Climbing beans will need a trellis or typee.

Beans, runner

'Phaseolus coccineus' from family 'Leguminosae'

Habit: Annual Aspect: Full sun to partial shade

Description: Climbing perennial bean from tropical America, having scarlet, pink or white flowers, grown until the 18th century as a garden ornamental but now cultivated largely for its long green edible pods and seeds

History: Grown by the Aztecs in subtropical highlands of Mexico and Guatemala, and in these regions before that for millennia.

Notes: A perennial in tropic climes.

GROWING GUIDE

Soil condition (conventional): Fertile, rich, well drained soil, sunny location

YeoPod mix (collar): JY1

YeoPod mix (cone): JY5

Propagation: From seed in modules indoors or in situ, after last frost date

Conventional spacing (inches): 18/9 (rows/in rows)

Spacing in YeoPod: 3 to 4 plants, subject to collar width

Days to pick: 84-98

Soil pH: 6.0-6.75

Plant yield: up to 3lb

Water: Ample and constant, when flowering

Seed life: 3 years

Ideal Germination Temperature: 80°F

Isolation: 800 yards

Optimum Growing Temperature: 60-70°F

Plant out date (weeks): 0

Seed germination: 7-14 days

Rotation: B

Intercrop: Climbing nasturtiums

Precede: Lettuce, Peas, early Potatoes, Radishes

To follow: Broccoli, Brussels sprouts, Cabbages, Cauliflowers, Collards, Kale, Kohlrabi

Comment: Keep roots constantly moist to ensure blossom set. Runners need tall sturdy supports.

Beetroot

Also known as Beet 'Beta vulgaris' from family 'Chenopodiaceae'

Habit: Biennial Aspect: Full sun to partial shade

Description: Related to sugar beet and mangel-wurzel, grown for its swollen root, typically red but also yellow or white, cooked to eat hot or cold in salads, or juiced. Leaves also edible when cooked.

History: Derives from northern Africa and the coasts of Spain and Portugal. Brought to northern Europe by the Romans as food for soldiers and horses. Red beetroot was developed by the Italians. Sugar beet developed by the Prussians in 1775.

GROWING GUIDE

Soil condition (conventional): Any, but ideally deep sandy fertile, not manured

YeoPod mix (collar): JY1

YeoPod mix (cone): JY5

Propagation: From seed sown in situ

Conventional spacing (inches): 10/6 (rows/in rows)

Spacing in YeoPod: 1 to 3 plants, subject to collar width

Days to pick: 78-112

Soil pH: 6.75-7.5

Plant yield: 5oz (globe), 8oz (long)

Water: Continuous watering avoids cracking

Seed life: 6 years

Ideal Germination Temperature: 85°F

Isolation: 3500 yards

Optimum Growing Temperature: 60-65°F

Plant out date (weeks): -6

Seed germination: 10-14 days

Rotation: D

Intercrop: Peas, Carrots (subject to collar width)

Precede: Lettuce, Radishes, Spring Onions

To follow: Garlic

Broccoli

Also known as Calabrese *'Brassica oleraceae'* from family *'Brassicaceae'*

Habit: Biennial **Aspect:** Sunny

Description: A variety of cabbage having branched green flower heads which are eaten before the flowers open. Broccoli sprouts can be cut throughout the season; calabrese typically forms a single head.

History: Derived from Kale, developed for market gardening in Italy around 1850 but first described in middle ages.

Notes: Calabrese (sprouting) crops in 12 weeks, purple & white (heading) varieties in 44 weeks. Fast growing varieties can be sown in traditional beds at 12in spacing in 12in rows.

GROWING GUIDE

Soil condition (conventional): Fertile, firm, rich soil, sunny location

YeoPod mix (collar): JY5

YeoPod mix (cone): JY7 or JY3

Propagation: From seed, usually sown in seedbed or flats

Conventional spacing (inches): 24/24

(max) (rows/in rows)

Spacing in YeoPod: one plant

Days to pick: 84

Soil pH: 6.0-7.5

Plant yield: 1.5lb

Water: Ample

Seed life: 5 years

Ideal Germination Temperature: 85°F

Isolation: 1600 yards

Optimum Growing Temperature: 60-65°F

Plant out date (weeks): -6

Seed germination: 7-12 days

Rotation: C

Intercrop: n/a

Precede: Lettuce, Radishes, Spring Onions

To follow: Beetroot, Carrots, Celeriac, Kohlrabi, Parsnip, Scorzonera

Brussels sprouts

'Brassica oleraceae v. gemmifera' from family 'Brassicaceae'

Habit: Biennial *Aspect:* Full sun to partial shade

Description: A variety of cabbage having a stout stem studded with bud-like heads resembling tiny cabbages, which are harvested from the base of the stem.

History: Derived from Kale. Developed only since 1750 in Belgium.

Notes: Early varieties mature in 28 weeks, late varieties in 36 weeks

GROWING GUIDE

Soil condition (conventional): Firm fertile drained soil, wind sheltered

YeoPod mix (collar): JY5

YeoPod mix (cone): JY7 or JY3

Propagation: From seed, usually sown in situ or seedbed or flats

Conventional spacing (inches): 6/30 (rows/in rows)

Spacing in YeoPod: one plant

Days to pick: 200

Soil pH: 6.0-7.5

Plant yield: 2lb

Water: Ample

Seed life: 5 years

Ideal Germination Temperature: 80°F

Isolation: 2000 yards

Optimum Growing Temperature: 60-65°F

Plant out date (weeks): -8

Seed germination: 7-12 days

Rotation: C

Intercrop: n/a

Precede: Lettuce, Radishes, Spring Onions

To follow: Beetroot, Carrots, Celeriac, Kohlrabi, Parsnip, Salsify, Scorzonera

Cabbage

Also known as Cole *'Brassica oleraceae v. capitata'* from family *'Brassicaceae'*

Habit: Biennial **Aspect:** Full sun to partial shade

Description: A cruciferous plant having a short thick stalk and a large, usually compact, head of green or red edible leaves. Closely related to broccoli, brussel sprouts, collards, kale and cauliflower.

History: Derived from Kale, in the coastlands of south-east Europe and the Channel Islands. Developed around BC500 by the Celts and, later, by the Romans. Introduced to America by Jacques Cartier in the 1600s.

Notes: Spring varieties mature in 35 weeks, others 20 to 35 weeks. Row width & conventional spacing are subject to the foliage canopy of the mature plant. Planting out times depend on variety. Brassica transplant well.

GROWING GUIDE

Soil condition (conventional): Firm, rich soil, manured in prior year, neutral to slightly acidic.

YeoPod mix (collar): JY5

YeoPod mix (cone): JY7 or JY3

Propagation: From seed, usually sown in situ or in seedbeds or flats

Conventional spacing (inches): 6/14 (min) (rows/in rows)

Spacing in YeoPod: one plant

Days to pick: 140-245

Soil pH: 6-7.5

Plant yield: 3/4lb-3lb

Water: Ample

Seed life: 5 years

Ideal Germination Temperature: 85°F

Isolation: 1600 yards

Optimum Growing Temperature: 60-65°F

Plant out date (weeks): -12

Seed germination: 7-12 days

Rotation: C

Intercrop: n/a

Precede: Lettuce, Radishes, Spring Onions

To follow: Garlic

Comment: different varieties of cabbage can be sown throughout Spring, Summer and Autumn. The above dates and successions apply to Summer cabbage varieties. Coat the roots of all brassica varieties in soot when transplanting, to deter club root.

Cabbage, chinese

Also known as Pak Choi *'Brassica chinensis'* from family *'Brassicaceae'*

Habit: Annual **Aspect:** Full sun to partial shade

Description: A Chinese plant closely related to cabbage and typically having crisp edible leaves growing in a loose cylindrical head.

History: Cultivated in China since 2000BC.

Notes: Many different varieties exist, some biennial. Chinese cabbage matures far faster than cabbage but some varieties are prone to early bolting.

GROWING GUIDE

Soil condition (conventional): Firm, fertile, needs ample nitrogen and water, neutral to slightly alkaline.

YeoPod mix (collar): JY7 or JY3

YeoPod mix (cone): JY7 or JY3

Propagation: see Cabbages

Conventional spacing (inches): 12/12 (rows/in rows)

Spacing in YeoPod: one plant

Days to pick: 42-84

Soil pH: 6.0-7.5

Plant yield: up to 2lb

Water: Copious and continuous

Seed life: 5 years

Ideal Germination Temperature: 75°F

Isolation: 1600 yards

Optimum Growing Temperature: 60-65°F

Plant out date (weeks): -4

Seed germination: 7-12 days

Rotation: C

Intercrop: n/a

Precede: Lettuce, Radishes, Spring Onions

To follow: Beetroot, Carrots, Celeriac, Kohlrabi, Parsnip, Salsify, Scorzonera

Carrots

'Daucus carota' from family 'Umbelliferae'

Habit: Biennial Aspect: Full sun to partial shade

Description: An umbelliferous plant with finely divided leaves, grown for its root - typically orange but sometimes yellow or purple, in cultivars of varying lengths. Usually cooked but also eaten raw in salads, or juiced.

History: Native to many regions. The first carrots were yellow and purple, introduced into western Europe from the Middle East in 10th century. Dutch growers in 17th century developed red carrots.

Notes: Early varieties mature in 12 weeks, maincrop in 16 weeks. Manure or stones cause roots to fang. Heavy rain may split roots.

GROWING GUIDE

Soil condition (conventional): Fine, deep, sandy loam, not recently manured

YeoPod mix (collar): JY1

YeoPod mix (cone): JY1

Propagation: From seed sown in situ. Tubers can also be started in degradeable pots then entire pot sunk in soil.

Conventional spacing (inches): 6/3 (rows/in rows)

Spacing in YeoPod: 3 to 4 plants, subject to collar width (one plant, if aiming for exhibition size)

Days to pick: 84-112

Soil pH: 6.0-6.75

Plant yield: 3oz (early), 6oz (maincrop)

Water: Steady watering, to avoid roots splitting

Seed life: 3 years

Ideal Germination Temperature: 80°F

Isolation: 500 yards

Optimum Growing Temperature: 60-65°F

Plant out date (weeks): -10

Seed germination: 17 days

Rotation: D

Intercrop: Peas, Salsify

Precede: Garlic, Lettuce, Peas

To follow: French beans

Cauliflowers

'*Brassica oleraceae v. botrytis*' from family '*Brassicaceae*'

Habit: Biennial **Aspect:** Full sun to partial shade

Description: A variety of cabbage having a large edible head of crowded white flowers on a short thick stem, eaten cooked or raw in salads.

History: Derives from Kale. Originated in Syria in 1000BC, used by the Romans, popular in Tudor times and called 'cole flower'.

Notes: Summer & autumn varieties mature in 126-168 days, winter varieties in 280-350 days. Mini varieties can be grown conventionally at 6in spacing in 6in rows.

GROWING GUIDE

Soil condition (conventional): Firm, well drained, deep, slightly alkaline, rich soil well watered.

YeoPod mix (collar): JY5

YeoPod mix (cone): JY7 or JY3

Propagation: Can be sown in situ or in modules or flats, then transplanted.

Conventional spacing (inches): 24/24 (max) (rows/in rows)

Spacing in YeoPod: one plant

Days to pick: see Notes

Soil pH: 5.5-7.5

Plant yield: 1-2lb

Water: Ample, continuous

Seed life: 5 years

Ideal Germination Temperature: 80°F

Isolation: 1600 yards

Optimum Growing Temperature: 60-65°F

Plant out date (weeks): -12

Seed germination: 7-12 days

Rotation: C

Intercrop: n/a

Precede: Cabbages, Peas, Radishes, Lettuce, Spring Onions

To follow: Garlic

Comment: Cauliflowers don't tolerate weeds.

Celeriac

'Apium graveolens v. rapaceum' from family 'Umbelliferae'

Habit: Biennial Aspect: Full sun to partial shade

Description: A variety of celery with a large turnip-like root, cooked or eaten raw shredded in salads.

History: Grown out of celery in the 17th century in Europe.

GROWING GUIDE

Soil condition (conventional): Fertile, moist, rich soil in sunny location

YeoPod mix (collar): JY3

YeoPod mix (cone): JY3 or JY3A

Propagation: Sow in degradeable pots in warmth, sunk in collar after last frost date

Conventional spacing (inches): 18/12 (rows/in rows)

Spacing in YeoPod: one plant

Days to pick: 210-245

Soil pH: 6.0-7.5

Plant yield: 10oz

Water: Copious

Seed life: 8 years

Ideal Germination Temperature: 70°F

Isolation: 500 yards

Optimum Growing Temperature: 60-65°F

Plant out date (weeks): 0

Seed germination: 12-18 days

Rotation: D

Intercrop: n/a

Precede: Peas, Potatoes,

To follow: (subsequent Spring) Potatoes

Celery

'Apium graveolens v. dulce' from family 'Umbelliferae'

Habit: Biennial Aspect: Full sun to partial shade

Description: An umbelliferous Eurasian plant whose leaf stalks, usually blanched, are eaten raw in salads or cooked.

History: Grew wild in salty soils and marshes, in many regions. Cultivated in France before the 16th century.

Notes: French varieties mature in 280 days, self-blanching varieties in 175 days

GROWING GUIDE

Soil condition (conventional): Deep, well drained, rich moist soil. Often grown in a trench, with well-rotted manure at base.

YeoPod mix (collar): JY1

YeoPod mix (cone): JY3 or JY3A

Propagation: From seed sown under glass and set out after last frost date

Conventional spacing (inches): 15/9 (rows/in rows)

Spacing in YeoPod: one plant

Days to pick: 280

Soil pH: 6.5-7.5

Plant yield: 12oz

Water: Copious and constant

Seed life: 8 years

Ideal Germination Temperature: 60°F

Isolation: 5000 yards

Optimum Growing Temperature: 60-65°F

Plant out date (weeks): 0

Seed germination: 12-18 days

Rotation: D

Intercrop: n/a

Precede: Peas, Potatoes

To follow: (in subsequent Spring) Potatoes

Comment: Transplants should be set in a half-filled collar and the collar earthed up as the plant grows

Collards

'*Brassica oleracea v. acephala*' from family '*Brassicaceae*'
Habit: Perennial *Aspect:* Full sun to partial shade

Description: A variety of cabbage, having a crown of edible leaves similar to kale but more drought and heat-resistant than kale, eaten cooked.

GROWING GUIDE

Soil condition (conventional): Rich, moist, well-drained soil with good nitrogen.

YeoPod mix (collar): JY5

YeoPod mix (cone): JY7 or JY3

Propagation: From seed, usually sown in situ or in seedbeds or flats

Conventional spacing (inches): 24/24 (rows/in rows)

Spacing in YeoPod: one plant

Days to pick: 84

Soil pH: 6-7.5

Plant yield: 3/4lb-3lb

Water: Ample

Seed life: 5 years

Ideal Germination Temperature: 85°F

Isolation: 1600 yards

Optimum Growing Temperature: 60-65°F

Plant out date (weeks): -12

Seed germination: 7-12 days

Rotation: C

Intercrop: n/a

Precede: Lettuce, Radishes, Spring Onions

To follow: n/a

Comment: Collards can often be grown as perennials, well mulched over Winter or the rootball taken indoors and kept in slightly damp sand, in darkness in a cool place.

Courgette

Also known as Zucchini, Marrow 'Cucurbita pepo' from family 'Cucurbitaceae'

Habit: Annual Aspect: Partial shade

Description: A small variety of vegetable marrow, typically green but also yellow, usually eaten cooked.

History: Courgettes belong to the squash family which originated in South America. Squash were eaten in Mexico as long ago as 8000BC. One of the earliest Indian food crops, squash spread throughout North America before the arrival of Columbus and appeared in Europe in the 16th century.

Notes: Large courgettes become Marrows, although seed varieties can be bought specifically to grow as Courgettes.

GROWING GUIDE

Soil condition (conventional): Very rich soil, continuously watered, ideally in planting hole with manure at base.

YeoPod mix (collar): JY5

YeoPod mix (cone): JY6 or JY3A

Propagation: From seed, usually indoors in degradeable pots set out after last frost date. Trailing varieties can be grown conventionally on mounds or ridges.

Conventional spacing (inches): 12/24 (rows/in rows)

Spacing in YeoPod: one plant

Days to pick: 70-98

Soil pH: 6.0-6.75

Plant yield: 16 fruits (4lb)

Water: Copious and constant

Seed life: 5 years

Ideal Germination Temperature: 95°F

Isolation: 800 yards

Optimum Growing Temperature: 65-75°F

Plant out date (weeks): 0

Seed germination: 5-8 days

Rotation: DX

Intercrop: n/a

Precede: short-rooted Carrots, Lettuce, Spring Onions, autumn-sown Garlic, Parsley

To follow: overWintering lettuce, chinese Cabbages

Comment: unless very wide collars are used, collars should be set out at 1 foot spacing between collar bases on either side to avoid shading

Garlic

Also known as Rocambole 'Allium sativum' from family

'Amaryllidaceae'

Habit: Biennial Aspect: Sunny Ideal Soil Type: Sandy Soil Moisture: Well drained

Description: A hardy Asian alliaceous plant with whitish flowers and a bulb comprised of small segments (cloves) with a strong taste and enduring odour, widely used in cooking.

History: Derived from mountains of central Asia, introduced to China by mongols, eaten in Pharonic Egypt and fed to workers on the pyramids.

Notes: Two varieties: *ssp ophioscorodon* (Rocambole) which throws up a snaking flower stalk, and *ssp sativum*, the more common form.

GROWING GUIDE

Soil condition (conventional): Light, well drained, fertile

YeoPod mix (collar): JY5

YeoPod mix (cone): JY5

Propagation: From cloves. Rarely yields fertile seed.

Conventional spacing (inches): 12/6 (rows/in rows)

Spacing in YeoPod: 1 -2 plants, subject to collar width

Days to pick: 168

Soil pH: 6.0-7.5

Plant yield: 3oz

Water: Minimal, except in drought

Seed life: n/a (cloves 8 months)

Ideal Germination Temperature: 60°F

Isolation: n/a

Optimum Growing Temperature: 50°F

Plant out date (weeks): -16 (Spring varieties). Hardneck overWintering garlic goes in +24 weeks ie. around November.

Seed germination: 10-20 days (Spring planted)

Rotation: B

Intercrop: n/a

Precede: none, Spring-started garlic goes in early.

To follow: Beetroot, Carrots, Celeriac, Kohlrabi, Parsnip, Salsify, Scorzonera

Comment: Should be vernalised (exposed to cold 32°F-50°F) for two months, eg. in fridge or in frosty ground, to develop large heads. Will not tolerate weeds.

Horseradish

'Ammoracia rusticana' from family *'Cruciferae'*

Habit: Perennial Aspect: Partial shade

Description: A coarse Eurasian plant grown for its thick pungent roots, shredded for use with cream, vinegar, etc as a condiment.

History: Native throughout Europe.

GROWING GUIDE

Soil condition (conventional): Any moist soil, any location. Winter hardy.

YeoPod mix (collar): JY4

YeoPod mix (cone): JY4

Propagation: Grown from root cuttings (thongs), best buried sideways. Rarely produces seed.

Conventional spacing (inches): 12/12 (rows/in rows)

Spacing in YeoPod: one plant

Days to pick: 80

Soil pH: 6.0-7.5

Plant yield: n/a

Water: Minimal

Seed life: n/a

Ideal Germination Temperature: 60°F

Isolation: n/a

Optimum Growing Temperature: 60-65°F

Plant out date (weeks): -12

Seed germination: n/a

Rotation: DX

Intercrop: n/a

Precede: n/a

To follow: n/a

Comment: Can become invasive as the smallest root fragment will grow. It is therefore well contained in a YeoPod, which should be its permanent home.

Kale

Also known as Borecole 'Brassica oleracea v. acephala' from family 'Brassicaceae'

Habit: Biennial Aspect: Full sun to partial shade

Description: A cultivated variety of cabbage, typically with green crinkled leaves but also smooth-leaved, renowned for its hardiness.

History: Closely related to the ancestor of the cabbage, sea kale, deriving from coasts of northern Europe. Of the same species as collards which thrives in heat, whereas kale prefers cool climes. First reference by Cato in 201BC.

Notes: Kale is very hardy and will usually overwinter despite frost.

GROWING GUIDE

Soil condition (conventional): Any soil, well drained, tolerates shade

YeoPod mix (collar): JY5

YeoPod mix (cone): JY7 or JY3

Propagation: From seeds sown in situ, or modules or flats. Also from cuttings.

Conventional spacing (inches): 6/18 (rows/in rows)

Spacing in YeoPod: one plant

Days to pick: 210-245

Soil pH: 6.0-6.75

Plant yield: 2lb

Water: Ample

Seed life: 5 years

Ideal Germination Temperature: 85°F

Isolation: 1600 yards

Optimum Growing Temperature: 60-65°F

Plant out date (weeks): -6

Seed germination: 7-12 days

Rotation: C

Intercrop: Peas, subject to collar width

Precede: Radishes, Lettuce, Spring onions

To follow: Potatoes (in subsequent year)

Kohlrabi

Also known as Turnip cabbage *'Brassica oleracea v. gongylodes'* from family *'Brassicaceae'*

Habit: Biennial Aspect: Full sun to partial shade

Description: A cultivated variety of cabbage, having a swollen lower stem eaten as a vegetable.

History: Derives from the cabbage (Europe) and first recorded around the 16th century.

GROWING GUIDE

Soil condition (conventional): Light, friable, sandy soil, well watered.

YeoPod mix (collar): JY1

YeoPod mix (cone): JY1

Propagation: From seed, sown in situ or in modules or flats

Conventional spacing (inches): 12/6 (rows/in rows)

Spacing in YeoPod: one plant

Days to pick: 56-84

Soil pH: 6.75

Plant yield: 1lb

Water: Ample

Seed life: 5 years

Ideal Germination Temperature: 85°F

Isolation: 1600 yards

Optimum Growing Temperature: 60-65°F

Plant out date (weeks): -12

Seed germination: 10 days

Rotation: C

Intercrop: n/a

Precede: Lettuce, Radishes, Spring Onions

To follow: Broad Beans, French Beans, Runner Beans

Leeks

'Allium ampeloprasum v. porrum' from family *'Amaryllidaceae'*

Habit: Biennial Aspect: Sunny

Description: A vegetable with a slender white bulb, cylindrical stem and broad flat overlapping leaves of a mild onion flavour, eaten cooked or shredded in salads.

History: Derives from Europe and

western Asia, and known to have been used for millennia.

Notes: Leeks are less troubled by pests and diseases than onions. Early varieties mature in 30 weeks, late varieties in 45 weeks. Multiplier leeks can be propagated by root division.

GROWING GUIDE

Soil condition (conventional): Any friable soil, well drained, sunny location.

YeoPod mix (collar): JY1

YeoPod mix (cone): JY4 or JY5

Propagation: From seed, sown in modules or flats. Seedlings when 8in high are sunk into 6in holes made with dibber and watered in.

Conventional spacing (inches): 12/6 (rows/in rows)

Spacing in YeoPod: 1 to 2 plants, subject to collar width (or up to 6 plants, if eaten when finger-thin)

Days to pick: 210-315

Soil pH: 6.75-7.5

Plant yield: 8oz

Water: Copious

Seed life: 3 years

Ideal Germination Temperature: 75°F

Isolation: 1600 yards

Optimum Growing Temperature: 55-75°F

Plant out date (weeks): -12

Seed germination: 14-18 days

Rotation: B

Intercrop: n/a

Precede: n/a

To follow: (in subsequent year) Broccoli, Brussels sprouts, Cabbages, Cauliflowers, Collards, Kale, Kohlrabi

Comments: leeks are best planted in a half-filled collar then earthed up as they grow. They may be blanched in tubes rolled from newspaper and secured with wire.

Lettuce

'Lactuca sativa' from family *'Asteraceae'*

Habit: Annual **Aspect:** Partial shade

Description: A wide genus of compositae cultivated for its large edible bunched leaves, typically green but also red or mottled, largely eaten raw in salads.

History: Derives from the Caucasus and western Asia. Known in Egypt in 4500BC and depicted on tomb walls. Cos lettuce was grown by the Romans and head lettuce introduced in the 16th century.

Notes: Cabbage & cos varieties mature in 8-14 weeks, looseleaf varieties in 6-8 weeks. A classic catchcrop between tall, slower maturing plants. Small Little Gem-type varieties need just 6in row space in conventional beds.

GROWING GUIDE

Soil condition (conventional): Moist, fertile, friable, neutral to slightly acidic. Lettuces tolerate shade

YeoPod mix (collar): JY5

YeoPod mix (cone): JY5

Propagation: From seed sown in situ, but can be transplanted from modules or flats.

Conventional spacing (inches): 12/12 (max) (rows/in rows)

Spacing in YeoPod: 1 cabbage variety, up to 4 small cos varieties, subject to collar width

Days to pick: 42-98

Soil pH: 6.0-7.5

Plant yield: 8oz

Water: Ample

Seed life: 3 years

Ideal Germination Temperature: 70°F (germination above 80°F is unreliable)

Isolation: 4 yards

Optimum Growing Temperature: 60-65°F

Plant out date (weeks): -10

Seed germination: 6-12 days

Rotation: DX

Intercrop: small lettuces may be used as intercrops for almost any fruit or vegetable, space permitting

Precede: anything

To follow: anything

Comment: according to variety, lettuces can be grown outdoors

year round - using cloches at the start and end of the year. They are very resistant to frost, having elastic cell walls, and even a plant frozen solid will often revive.

Melons

Also known as Musk melon, Water melon (though watermelons are of a different family) *'Cucumis melo'* from family *'Cucurbitaceae'*

Habit: Annual *Aspect:* Sunny

Description: A trailing plant grown for its edible fruit, having a hard rind and juicy flesh.

History: Derives from tropical western Africa and also Iran. Brought to southern Europe around 1st century BC. Not related to watermelons *(Citrullus lanatus).*

GROWING GUIDE

Soil condition (conventional): Rich, manured, deep, well-drained, sunny, very moist soil. Usually grown in temperate climes under glass.

YeoPod mix (collar): JY5

YeoPod mix (cone): JY6 or JY3A

Propagation: From seed, sown in modules.

Conventional spacing (inches): 36/36 (rows/in rows)

Spacing in YeoPod: one plant

Days to pick: 90

Soil pH: 5.5-6.5

Plant yield: 4 fruits

Water: Copious and constant

Seed life: 5 years

Ideal Germination Temperature: 85°F

Isolation: 800 yards

Optimum Growing Temperature: 65-75°F

Plant out date (weeks): 0

Seed germination: 6-9 days

Rotation: A

Intercrop: n/a

Precede: Lettuce, Spring Onions

To follow: overWintering Chinese Cabbage, Lettuce

Comment: In temperate climes, melons will ripen only under glass except in very favoured locations. They are best grown in a greenhouse and, if it's solidly-floored, in a collar set on a GrowBag.

Onions

'Allium cepa' from family 'Amaryllidaceae'

Habit: Biennial **Aspect:** Sunny

Description: An alliaceous plant having greenish white flowers, grown for its edible bulb of pungent taste and odour. Japanese or bunching onions yield clusters of small bulbs at the top of the stem.

History: From southern Russia and Iran. Much eaten by the ancient Egyptians.

Notes: Onions do not tolerate weeds. Sets mature in 20 weeks. Seed-sown onions mature in 46 weeks if sown in August or 22 weeks if sown in Spring.

GROWING GUIDE

Soil condition (conventional): Fertile, well drained, sunny, manured in prior year. Must be kept weed-free.

YeoPod mix (collar): JY5

YeoPod mix (cone): JY5

Propagation: Most easily grown from sets. Onions grown from seed need a richer, more friable mix (eg. JY4) than those grown from sets.

Conventional spacing (inches): 9/4 (rows/ in rows)

Spacing in YeoPod: 1 to 4 plants, subject to collar width

Days to pick: 140

Soil pH: 6.0-7.5

Plant yield: 4oz-8oz

Water: Minimal, except in drought

Seed life: 1-2 years

Ideal Germination Temperature: 75°F

Isolation: 1600 yards

Optimum Growing Temperature: 55-75°F

Plant out date (weeks): -16 (sets)

Seed germination: 11-14 days

Rotation: B

Intercrop: Beetroot, Lettuce, Carrots

Precede: n/a

To follow: Cabbages, Lettuce, Broad Beans, French Beans

Comment: Four onion seeds can be sown in one module and the intertwined young plants set out in a collar as one plant. This will form four bulbs of normal size.

Parsnip

'Pastinaca sativa' from family *'Umbelliferae'*

Habit: Biennial **Aspect:** Full sun to partial shade

Description: An umbelliferous plant cultivated for its long edible whitish root, usually eaten cooked.

History: Derives from eurasia and much used in Britain in the middle ages before being supplanted by the potato.

Growing Guide

Soil condition (conventional): Friable, sandy, deep, manure-free, stone-free, fertile

YeoPod mix (collar): JY1

YeoPod mix (cone): JY1

Propagation: From seed, usually sown in situ but tubers can be started in degradeable pots then sunk in collar.

Conventional spacing (inches): 12/6 (rows/ in rows)

Spacing in YeoPod: 1 to 4 plants, subject to collar width

Days to pick: 238

Soil pH: 6.0-7.5

Plant yield: 6oz

Water: Minimal, except in drought

Seed life: 1 years

Ideal Germination Temperature: 65°F

Isolation: 1600 yards

Optimum Growing Temperature: 60-65°F

Plant out date (weeks): -16

Seed germination: 10-28 days

Rotation: D

Intercrop: n/a

Precede: n/a

To follow: (subsequent year) Onions, Peas, Potatoes, Shallots

Comment: Keep the roots in the soil during frost to sweeten the flavour.

Peas

Also known as English peas *'Pisum sativum'* from family *'Leguminosae'*

Habit: Annual **Aspect:** Partial shade

Description: An annual climbing vegetable of various heights, having small white flowers and long green pods, both pods and seeds usually being edible. Not to be confused with Field peas (Crowders), which don't crop in temperate climes, or Sweet peas (flowers) which are inedible.

History: Often called English peas in America, to distinguish them from crowder or field peas *(Vigna unguiculata)*. Eaten in the Bronze Age and found in the city of Troy. Originated in eastern Mediterranean.

Notes: Peas are often sown in double rows, the rows 3in apart, against chicken wire (bush varieties). Climbing varieties need a trellis. Round-seed peas can be sown outdoors in Winter (but are vulnerable to rot). Best is to sow wrinkled peas in Spring.

GROWING GUIDE

Soil condition (conventional): Fertile, friable, low in nitrogen but with good potassium (potash), well-watered, cool location. Tolerates shade.

YeoPod mix (collar): JY5

YeoPod mix (cone): JY5 or JY4

Propagation: From seed, usually sown in situ. But can be grown in modules.

Conventional spacing (inches): 18/2 (rows/in rows)

Spacing in YeoPod: 4 to 6 plants, subject to collar width

Days to pick: 84-112

Soil pH: 6.0-7.5

Plant yield: Shelled: 3oz (dwarf), up to 1lb (climbing)

Water: Modest, except in drought.

Seed life: 3 years

Ideal Germination Temperature: 75°F

Isolation: 15 yards

Optimum Growing Temperature: 60-65°F

Plant out date (weeks): -12

Seed germination: 7-10 days

Rotation: B

Intercrop: n/a

Precede: n/a

To follow: Broad Beans, French Beans, Runner Beans

Comment: Climbing peas will need a trellis or typee. Dwarf peas will benefit from a short cage erected around the collar rim, which will furthermore deter birds. But dwarf peas can also be allowed to trail down over the collar.

Peppers, sweet

Also known as Capsicums *'Capsicum annum'* from family *'Solanaceae'*

Habit: Annual **Aspect:** Sunny

Description: A mild flavoured tropical plant having hollow red, green or yellow fruits eaten cooked or raw in salads. Not to be confused with Chilli peppers *(C. frutescens)* - a closely related Capsicum with hot-tasting flesh and seeds, used as flavourings. Or with the pepper plant *Piper nigrum*, which yields black peppercorns. All are perennial in warm climes.

History: Chilli peppers originated in Bolivia, but wild peppers extended as far north as the southern US states. They were brought to Europe by Columbus then distributed via the Portugese trade routes to China in the 16th century. The Hungarians were referring to them as paprika as early as 1569.

GROWING GUIDE

Soil condition (conventional): Very rich, moist soil, neutral to slightly acidic, warm location, best grown in temperate climes under glass.

YeoPod mix (collar): JY5

YeoPod mix (cone): JY3A or JY6

Propagation: From seed, usually sown in modules in warmth

Conventional spacing (inches): 18/18 (rows/in rows)

Spacing in YeoPod: one plant

Days to pick: 126

Soil pH: 6-7.5

Plant yield: 6-10 fruits

Water: Copious, when fruiting

Seed life: 3 years

Ideal Germination Temperature: 85°F

Isolation: 200 yards

Optimum Growing Temperature: 70-75°F

Plant out date (weeks): 0

Seed germination: 14-21 days

Rotation: DX

Intercrop: n/a

Precede: stub-rooted Carrots, Garlic, Parsley

To follow: overWintering Lettuce, chinese Cabbage

Comment: Sweet peppers fruit unreliably outdoors in temperate climes. They are best grown in a greenhouse eg. in a collar set atop a GrowBag.

Potatoes

'*Solanum tuberosum*' from family '*Solanaceae*'

Habit: Annual *Aspect:* Full sun to partial shade

Description: A South American plant grown for its edible tubers, typically white-fleshed but also yellow, red or black, eaten cooked. The seed clusters and leaves are poisonous. Not to be confused with Sweet potatoes.

History: Derives from the Andes and cultivated for 8000 years. Brought from Virginia to Britain by Sir Francis Drake in 16th century.

Notes: Potatoes are not roots but actually vine fruits. They'll grow happily up a wall, like melons, if supported. And potato breeders grow them that way. Early varieties mature in 13 weeks, maincrops in 22 weeks.

GROWING GUIDE

Soil condition (conventional): Any fertile soil, lime-free, manured in previous year, slightly acidic.

YeoPod mix (collar): JY2 or JY4

YeoPod mix (cone): JY6

Propagation: From tubers, usually chitted (pre-sprouted) indoors in warmth. However, seed - from seed heads - can also be sown in warmth in degradeable pots.

Conventional spacing (inches): 30/15 (maincrop) (rows/in rows)

Spacing in YeoPod: one plant

Days to pick: 91-154

Soil pH: 5.25-6.0

Plant yield: 1.5lb (early)-3lb (maincrop)

Water: Minimal, except in drought

Seed life: 8 months (seed potato); 1 year (seed)

Ideal Germination Temperature: 65°F

Isolation: n/a

Optimum Growing Temperature: 60-65°F

Plant out date (weeks): -10

Seed germination: n/a

Rotation: A

Intercrop: Parsley, Spring Onions

Precede: n/a

To follow: anything whatever, apt to its season

Comment: Potatoes need a lot of space. Use a very large YeoPod or stack two collars on top of each other to form a pagoda - held secure with canes rammed deep at each four angles. Plant one chitted potato in the bottom collar, half filled with soil mix. Continue to earth it up as the foliage emerges. Then add a second collar, and continue to earth it up.

Note: Wrap seed potatoes in grass clippings, comfrey leaves or *any* green leaf. This deters scab.

Pumpkins

'Cucurbita pepo' from family *'Cucurbitaceae'*

Habit: Annual *Aspect:* Full sun to partial shade

Description: A trailing plant that yields large fruit usually ovoid and orange, having a thick rind and pulpy flesh, eaten cooked. The toasted seeds are also edible.

History: From the Andean valleys and northern Argentina.

GROWING GUIDE

Soil condition (conventional): Very rich, continually moist, well drained soil in warm location.

YeoPod mix (collar): JY5

YeoPod mix (cone): JY6 or JY3A

Propagation: see Courgette

Conventional spacing (inches): 48/24 (rows/in rows)

Spacing in YeoPod: one plant

Days to pick: 70-98

Soil pH: 6.0-6.75

Plant yield: 2-3 fruits

Water: see Courgette

Seed life: 6 years

Ideal Germination Temperature: 95°F

Isolation: 800 yards

Optimum Growing Temperature: 65-75°F

Plant out date (weeks): 0

Seed germination: 5-8 days

Rotation: A

Intercrop: n/a

Precede: Lettuce, Peas, Radishes

To follow: overWintering Lettuce, chinese Cabbage

Comment: Pumpkins notoriously need a lot of lateral space. So for large pumpkins, position the YeoPods at least two foot apart (more, if you're growing giants). Even small squash will benefit from a one foot spacing.

Radishes

'Raphanus sativus' from family 'Brassicaceae'

Habit: Annual Aspect: Full sun to partial shade

Description: An Eurasian plant grown for its small crisp red root with white flesh, usually eaten raw in salads. Leaves and pods are also edible. Large Asian or Winter varieties of various skin colours can also be cooked.

History: Derives from the middle east and Asia. Pictured on pyramid walls in Egypt and in Mediterranean artwork dating to

2000BC.

Notes: Winter radishes are biennial.

GROWING GUIDE

Soil condition (conventional): Any soil, fertile, moist, well-drained, but prefers light sandy soil.

YeoPod mix (collar): JY1

YeoPod mix (cone): JY1

Propagation: From seed, sown in situ

Conventional spacing (inches): 6/1 (rows/in rows)

Spacing in YeoPod: 4-10 plants, subject to collar width

Days to pick: 21-42

Soil pH: 6.0-7.5

Plant yield: 30 plants yield around 1lb

Water: Meagre but continuous

Seed life: 5 years

Ideal Germination Temperature: 85°F

Isolation: 800 yards

Optimum Growing Temperature: 60-65°F

Plant out date (weeks): -12

Seed germination: 4-7 days

Rotation: DX (can be sown anywhere)

Intercrop: Radishes can be used as an intercrop to Beetroot, Broad Beans, Broad Beans, Broad Beans, Carrots, Chervil, Cucumbers, Cucumbers, French Beans, Lettuce, Nasturtiums, Parsnip, Peas, Runner Beans, Spinach, Bananas and Pineapples

Precede: n/a

To follow: n/a

Rhubarb

'Rheum rhabarbarum' from family 'Polygonaceae'

Habit: Perennial Aspect: Full sun to partial shade

Description: A perennial hardy plant having large leaves and long green-and-red acidic stalks, edible when cooked and sweetened. The leaves themselves are poisonously high in oxalic acid.

History: From the more temperate regions of Asia. Brought to Europe by early explorers.

GROWING GUIDE

Soil condition (conventional): Any rich soil, well-drained, sunny location, manured. Tolerates some shade.

YeoPod mix (collar): JY3 or JY3A or JY6

YeoPod mix (cone): JY3 or JY3A or JY6

Propagation: Best grown from mature roots (crowns) divided and re-planted every five years, though growing from seed under glass is possible.

Conventional spacing (inches): 36/36 (rows/in rows)

Spacing in YeoPod: one plant

Days to pick: 400

Soil pH: 5.25-6.75

Plant yield: 5lb

Water: Minimal, except in drought

Seed life: 1 year

Ideal Germination Temperature: n/a

Isolation: n/a

Optimum Growing Temperature: 30-60°F

Plant out date (weeks): -12

Seed germination: n/a

Rotation: DX

Intercrop: n/a

Precede: n/a (Rhubarb emerges very early)

To follow: overWintering Lettuce, chinese Cabbage (when the rhubarb has died back)

Comment: Rhubarb is not the best candidate for a YeoPod as it will grow almost anywhere, especially in acid soil. Each plant - like Horseradish - should have a YeoPod to itself, in perpetuity.

Salsify

Also known as Oyster plant, Vegetable oyster 'Tragopogon porrifolius' from family 'Asteraceae'

Habit: Biennial Aspect: Sunny

Description: A Mediterranean plant having grass-like leaves, purple flower heads and a long white thin edible taproot, eaten cooked and said to taste like oysters.

History: From southern Europe, where still grows wild. Cultivated in Italy from 13th century. Also called vegetable Oyster.

GROWING GUIDE

Soil condition (conventional): Deep, sandy, friable, stone-free. Not recently manured.

YeoPod mix (collar): JY1

YeoPod mix (cone): JY1

Propagation: From seed, sown in situ or in degradeable pots.

Conventional spacing (inches): 12/6 (rows/in rows)

Spacing in YeoPod: 1 to 4 plants, subject to collar width

Days to pick: 175

Soil pH: 6.75

Plant yield: 3oz

Water: Minimal

Seed life: 4 years

Ideal Germination Temperature: 75°F

Isolation: 500 yards

Optimum Growing Temperature: 55-75°F

Plant out date (weeks): -12

Seed germination: 12-16 days

Rotation: D

Intercrop: n/a

Precede: n/a

To follow: (subsequent year) Potatoes

Scorzonera

Also known as Black salsify *'Scorzonera hispanica'* from family *'Asteraceae'*

Habit: Biennial *Aspect:* Sunny

Description: A European vegetable similar to Salsify but with a black skin, grown for its long, thin edible taproot and eaten cooked.

History: Derives from southern Europe.

GROWING GUIDE

Soil condition (conventional): Deep, sandy, friable, stone-free. Not recently manured.

YeoPod mix (collar): JY1

YeoPod mix (cone): JY1

Propagation: see Salsify

Conventional spacing (inches): see Salsify (rows/in rows)

Spacing in YeoPod: see Salsify

Days to pick: 175

Soil pH: 6.75

Plant yield: 3oz

Water: Minimal

Seed life: 2 years

Ideal Germination Temperature: 75°F

Isolation: 500 yards

Optimum Growing Temperature: 55-75°F

Plant out date (weeks): -12

Seed germination: 12-16 days

Rotation: D

Intercrop: n/a

Precede: n/a

To follow: (subsequent year) Potatoes

Shallots

Also known as Scallions. *'Allium ascalonicum'* from family *'Amaryllidaceae'*

Habit: Biennial *Aspect*: Sunny

Description: An alliaceous plant grown for its small edible bulb which divides into sections and is cooked in the manner of a mild-tasting onion, or pickled.

History: Shallots have a history as ancient as onions, and similar to it. The Greeks and Romans believed that shallots came from Ascalon in Palestine - hence the name 'scallions'.

GROWING GUIDE

Soil condition (conventional): Fertile, well drained, sunny, manured in prior year. Must be kept weed-free.

YeoPod mix (collar): JY5

YeoPod mix (cone): JY5

Propagation: From sets. Each bulb yields a cluster of small further bulbs.

Conventional spacing (inches): 9/6 (rows/in rows)

Spacing in YeoPod: 1 to 4 cloves, subject to collar width

Days to pick: 126

Soil pH: 6.0-6.75

Plant yield: 3oz

Water: Minimal, except in drought

Seed life: 1-2 years

Ideal Germination Temperature: 75°F

Isolation: 1600 yards

Optimum Growing Temperature: 55-75°F

Plant out date (weeks): -16

Seed germination: 11-14 days

Rotation: B

Intercrop: n/a

Precede: n/a

To follow: Lettuce, or almost anything except Beans

Spinach

'Spinacia oleracea' from family *'Chenopodiaceae'*

Habit: Annual *Aspect*: Partial shade

Description: An annual plant grown for its dark green edible leaves, usually eaten boiled or steamed. Not to be confused with New Zealand spinach or perpetual spinach (Spinach beet), which have similar flavour but are unrelated.

History: Derives from many parts of Asia. Came to China in 7th century and to Spain in 12th century.

GROWING GUIDE

Soil condition (conventional): Rich, fertile, well drained, tolerates shade.

YeoPod mix (collar): JY5

YeoPod mix (cone): JY5

Propagation: From seed, sown in situ or modules or flats.

Conventional spacing (inches): 12/3 (rows/in rows)

Spacing in YeoPod: one plant

Days to pick: 56-98

Soil pH: 6.75-7.5

Plant yield: up to 8oz

Water: Copious

Seed life: 5 years

Ideal Germination Temperature: 70°F

Isolation: 8000 yards

Optimum Growing Temperature: 60-65°F

Plant out date (weeks): -12

Seed germination: 12-20 days

Rotation: D

Intercrop: n/a

Precede: n/a

To follow: Anything whatsoever

Squash

'Cucurbita pepo' from family 'Cucurbitaceae'

Habit: Annual Aspect: Sunny

Description: A wide genus of trailing marrow-like plants bearing fruits of many shapes and colours, having a hard rind and edible flesh, eaten cooked. Flowers of some cultivars are also edible.

History: Derives from North and South America.

GROWING GUIDE

Soil condition (conventional): Very rich soil, continuously watered, ideally in planting hole with manure at base.

YeoPod mix (collar): JY5

YeoPod mix (cone): JY6 or JY3A

Propagation: see Courgette

Conventional spacing (inches): 48/24 (rows/in rows)

Spacing in YeoPod: one plant

Days to pick: 70-98

Soil pH: 6.0-6.75

Plant yield: enormous

Water: see Courgette

Seed life: 6 years

Ideal Germination Temperature: 95°F

Isolation: 800 yards

Optimum Growing Temperature: 65-75°F

Plant out date (weeks): 0

Seed germination: 5-8 days

Rotation: A

Intercrop: n/a

Precede: stub-rooted Carrots, winter-planted Garlic, Parsley

To follow: (subsequent year) Broad Beans

Comment: Trailing squash will need a large YeoPod and ample space.

Strawberries

'Fragaria x ananassa' from family *'Rosaceae'*

Habit: Perennial **Aspect:** Sunny

Description: A low-growing rosaceous bush, of both trailing and small alpine varieties, having red edible fruits normally propagated by runners.

History: The only fruit that bears its seeds on its skin.

Notes: Perpetuate from runners and discard old roots after three years.

GROWING GUIDE

Soil condition (conventional): Deep, well drained, fertile, manure-rich, acidic

YeoPod mix (collar): JY5 (omitting lime)

YeoPod mix (cone): JY6 or JY3A

Propagation: Usually from runners in late Summer, though production from seed is possible.

Conventional spacing (inches): 36/18 (rows/in rows)
Alpine varieties can be grown 12/12.

Spacing in YeoPod: 1 plant, (alpine varieties up to four plants subject to collar width)

Days to pick: n/a

Soil pH: 5.25-6.0

Plant yield: 8oz

Water: Constant, when fruiting

Seed life: n/a

Ideal Germination Temperature: n/a

Isolation: n/a

Optimum Growing Temperature: 65-75°F

Plant out date (weeks): 12

Seed germination: n/a

Rotation: DX

Intercrop: Onions (subject to collar width)

Precede: Spring Onions

To follow: overWintering Lettuce

Swedes

Also known as Rutabaga, Swedish turnip *'Brassica napus'* from family *'Brassicaceae'*

Habit: Biennial **Aspect:** Full sun to partial shade

Description: An Eurasian plant of the cabbage family grown for its edible bulbous root, eaten cooked.

History: Brassica napus. First recorded in Lapland in 1500. A different species from Turnips *(Brassica campestris).*

GROWING GUIDE

Soil condition (conventional): Firm, rich, moist.

YeoPod mix (collar): JY7

YeoPod mix (cone): JY7

Propagation: From seed, sown in situ or in modules or flats.

Conventional spacing (inches): 15/9 (rows/

in rows)

Spacing in YeoPod: 1 plant

Days to pick: 140-168

Soil pH: 6.0-6.75

Plant yield: up to 2.5lb

Water: Ample, to avoid woody roots.

Seed life: 5 years

Ideal Germination Temperature: 85°F

Isolation: 1600 yards

Optimum Growing Temperature: 60-65°F

Plant out date (weeks): -6

Seed germination: 6-10 days

Rotation: C

Intercrop: n/a

Precede: Lettuce, Radishes, Spring Onions

To follow: Lettuce, (subsequent year) Broad Beans, French Beans

Sweet corn

Also known as Maize *'Zea mays'* from family *'Gramineae'*

Habit: Annual Aspect: Sunny

Description: A variety of maize with stems up to 8 foot and sugar-rich kernels, eaten cooked and also dried to grind as a flour. Not to be confused with Corn, a term applied in Britain to a cereal crop.

History: Derives from the Andes. Used by the Incas, Aztecs and North American indians. Introduced to Europe by Columbus in the 16th century and to Africa earlier than this.

GROWING GUIDE

Soil condition (conventional): Fertile, deep, well drained, neutral to slightly acidic.

YeoPod mix (collar): JY5

YeoPod mix (cone): JY6 or JY3A

Propagation: From seed, best sown in degradeable pots. Set out in blocks of four or more plants to ensure cross-pollination.

Conventional spacing (inches): 14/14 (rows/in rows)

Spacing in YeoPod: one plant

Days to pick: 98

Soil pH: 6.5

Plant yield: 2 cobs

Water: Copious, at flowering time

Seed life: 3 years

Ideal Germination Temperature: 95°F

Isolation: 3200 yards

Optimum Growing Temperature: 60-75°F

Plant out date (weeks): 0

Seed germination: 10-12 days

Rotation: A

Intercrop: n/a

Precede: Peas, Lettuce, Spring Onions, stub-rooted Carrots

To follow: any overWintering plant

Swiss chard

Also known as Chard, Leaf beet
'*Beta vulgaris v. cycla*' from family
'*Chenopodiaceae*'

Habit: Biennial *Aspect*: Full sun to
partial shade

Description: A variety of beet grown
for its large succulent leaves and
thick stalks, both eaten cooked.

History: Related to Beetroot.

GROWING GUIDE

Soil condition (conventional): Rich, well
manured, nitrogenous, tolerates
some shade

YeoPod mix (collar): JY5

YeoPod mix (cone): JY6 or JY3A

Propagation: From seed, usually in
situ.

Conventional spacing (inches): 15/12
(rows/in rows)

Spacing in YeoPod: one plant

Days to pick: 84

Soil pH: 6.75

Plant yield: 1lb

Water: Ample, continuous

Seed life: 6 years

Ideal Germination Temperature: 85°F

Isolation: 3500 yards

Optimum Growing Temperature: 60-
65°F

Plant out date (weeks): -12

Seed germination: 10-14 days

Rotation: D

Intercrop: n/a

Precede: Lettuce, Radishes, Spring

Onions

To follow: Broad Beans, French
Beans, (subsequent year) Potatoes

Tomatoes

'*Lycopersicon Lycopersicon*' from
family '*Solanaceae*'

Habit: Annual *Aspect*: Sunny

Description: A South American plant
with cultivars of various heights
grown for its fleshy fruits, typically
red when mature but also yellow,
pink, orange, green or purple. Eaten
cooked or raw in salads.

History: Originated in south America
and domesticated in Mexico and
central America. Brought to Europe
by Columbus and initially thought
poisonous.

Notes: Ultra-early varieties may
fruit in 10 weeks, beefsteak and
late varieties in 16 weeks.
Tomatoes are perennials in the
tropics. All varieties need staking,
even bush, if only to deter slugs.
Remove suckers (shoots between
leaf and stem). These can be
transplanted, early in the season.

GROWING GUIDE

Soil condition (conventional): Rich, deep,
well drained, moist, sunny warm
location

YeoPod mix (collar): JY5

YeoPod mix (cone): JY6 or JY3A or
JY3

Propagation: From seed, sown in

modules or degradeable pots and set out after last frost date.

Conventional spacing (inches): 30/18 (rows/in rows)

Spacing in YeoPod: one plant

Days to pick: 70-112

Soil pH: 6.0

Plant yield: 4lb

Water: Constant, as soon as fruits set

Seed life: 4 years

Ideal Germination Temperature: 85°F

Isolation: 1 yards (most varieties)

Optimum Growing Temperature: 70-75°F

Plant out date (weeks): 0

Seed germination: 8-11 days

Rotation: A

Intercrop: n/a

Precede: stub-rooted Carrots, Garlic, Parsley, Lettuce

To follow: overWintering Lettuce, chinese Cabbage

Turnips

'Brassica rapa rapa' from family *'Brassicaceae'*

Habit: Biennial *Aspect:* Partial shade

Description: A member of the cabbage family, having a large yellow or white edible root, normally eaten cooked.

History: Came from Europe and much used by the Gauls, Romans and Germanic tribes. A different species from Swedes or Rutabagas *(Brassica napus).*

Notes: Early varieties can be grown 5 inches apart in rows 9 inches apart. Turnips planted in Autumn are biennial.

GROWING GUIDE

Soil condition (conventional): Fertile, firm, non-acid, sandy or friable, well drained, no manure

YeoPod mix (collar): JY1

YeoPod mix (cone): JY5

Propagation: From seed, usually sown in situ.

Conventional spacing (inches): 12/9 (maincrop) (rows/in rows)

Spacing in YeoPod: 1 to 3 plants, subject to collar width

Days to pick: 42-84

Soil pH: 6.0-7.5

Plant yield: 12oz (maincrop)

Water: Ample, to avoid woody roots

Seed life: 5 years

Ideal Germination Temperature: 85°F

Isolation: 1600 yards

Optimum Growing Temperature: 60-65°F

Plant out date (weeks): -12

Seed germination: 6-10 days

Rotation: C

Intercrop: n/a

Precede: n/a

To follow: Broad Beans, French Beans, Lettuce

If you liked *The Lazy Vegetable Grower*, you'll *love* the Village Guild!

Discover the secrets of growing *more* fresh, healthy, organic food at your home - with *less* work, land or money than you ever thought possible

Dear Fellow Lazy Gardener

May I invite you to join us as a Charter member of the Village Guild?

We're a little association of folk just like you and me who enjoy growing our own vegetables, fruit and flowers - and trying odd things in our gardens. But we hate the unreal nonsense of those television programmes and 'coffee table' gardening books where everything is perfect, no weed is ever seen nor any leaf is chewed by slugs (but only after a 24 hour makeover!).

We're *real* gardeners. And you and I know that real gardens *aren't like that.*

The best of the world's *real* gardening ideas

Instead, may I share with you the best of the world's *real* gardening ideas - brilliant, ingenious and often downright 'whacky-but-they-work' secrets developed by folk just like you and me from our own experience - for growing more and better plants? Most involve little or no labour, and some even demand little or no soil!

And may I also show you what I've *personally* tested - from my 31 years in organic gardening and research, and that works bountifully in my garden year round, and that you can do right now (even if you don't have a garden)?

Gardening should be fun, and so is the Guild

Frankly, I retired a few years ago and started the Village Guild for fun plus - hopefully - a little revenue to pay my wife's hairdressing bills... (enough said).

So largely for fun (mine and yours) let me show you from my real down-to-earth triumphs and mistakes... how to grow *more* healthy organic food - whether vegetables, salads, fruits or herbs - than you can easily imagine. Sustainably, and without chemical fertilisers or pesticides.

Using these ideas, you'll do it effortlessly. Just as I do...

~ With **less work**, or none (and I speak as an unashamedly lazy man. I have a short attention span plus back problems. I can't dig or lift. So if something's boring or not easy, *I don't do it*.)

~ For **very little money**, or no money at all. (Indeed, I've proven you can *make* money from the smallest garden - cash in hand - even if like me you're retired and living on a modest fixed income. I'll show you how.)

~ And you'll **enjoy** your gardening so much more.

(When *The Independent* newspaper ran a wonderful one-third page article on the Village Guild, its photographer exclaimed, in so many words: "That's genius! I didn't know you could do all those clever things in Britain. It makes me want to garden myself..." Of course, you can do "all those clever things", in Britain or anywhere else, *and I'll show you how*. Step by step.)

Rediscover long-forgotten gardening lore, and gain extraordinary harvests

In centuries past, it was considered no trick to grow 15kg of potatoes from one seed, or produce fresh home-grown peas, dwarf beans or pineapples on Christmas Day.

Now I've updated and tested those ideas using not only my garden but also... my patio, greenhouse, garage, even windowsill - so you can replicate such miracles all by yourself, even in the depths of a city. And with *less* work than those old head gardeners would ever have believed possible.

What's more, you'll also:

~Prove for yourself how easy it is to be **self-sufficient** in food on even the tiniest plot. Yes, you *can* feed a family of five for less than £20 a year, in all the fresh-food vitamins they'll need.

~ Enjoy **home health remedies** that really work. You can throw away many of the costly pills and potions in your medicine cabinet. Simply grow your own simple remedies for common family ailments in your garden! I've personally proven they work, astoundingly well. And most are free.

~Make your own **cosmetics, deodorants, cleaning aids, pest repellants** plus every manner of **household** and **personal hygiene** products. I've used them for years. They're often better - and safer - than the heavily advertised supermarket brands. They certainly cost a lot less! And you'll usually find them no further away than your garden or grocery cupboard.

~ Take a new **pride** and **confidence** in your own gardening skills. Chances are, you're already doing a lot more right than you thought. It may take just a clever tweak or two to your existing methods to *multiply* your yield of healthy fresh produce - manyfold. My *Lazy Gardener* newsletter - yours when you join the Guild - gives you literally thousands of these no-nonsense tested ideas to maximise your results.

Where do these novel ideas come from?

Many have been closely guarded by commercial growers, sometimes for centuries. They've never been divulged before. (How did I find them, in totally legal and ethical ways? *I'll tell you, when you join us!*)

Other breakthrough ideas have been developed by folk like you and me all over the world, from personal experiments in our own gardens. But usually we've passed them on only to our families and friends. I've spent three decades compiling them, at no little cost - by subscribing to every little known *practical* gardening newsletter or resource I could find on this planet!

Now they're yours. All of them, when you join us as a Charter member.

What exactly do you receive?

1. You receive a giant idea-packed newsletter

For a start, you get my giant newsletter *The Lazy Gardener* every two months. Each is often as big as a small novel and, I promise you, is more entertaining than most novels! (You can take it on holiday and still not have finished it by the time you've spent all your traveller's cheques.)

What it *doesn't* contain is lots of pretty colour pictures, though it's profusely illustrated. (Have you noticed, editors put big pictures into gardening magazines largely to fill up space?) Instead, it's packed with clever "do them now because they work" gardening *ideas*.

These can range from simple but intensely useful tips, such as:

* how to grow four successive crops of potatoes in one tiny plot in one season, or * make just one square foot of garden yield you 20lb of healthy edible produce in eight months, or * grow a tomato plant that will fill your entire freezer with tomato paste and juice - from just one plant.

Or even previously unheard-of ways to...

* make slugs do your weeding for you (while leaving your favourite plants alone); * grow potatoes that "earth up" themselves; * make cats scat from your seedbed using an old sock and a cola bottle; * repel carrot fly - without onions or barriers; * eliminate cutworms, nematodes, caterpillars and just about any other pest you can name - organically, without work or chemicals. * *Plus thousands more, original problem-solving tips.*

You'll also explore complete *strategic* gardening plans.

For example:

~Try the fabled Asian system of **Ayurvedic** gardening (I've remodelled it for Western gardens, so it works in even the smallest allotment)... and you may never again need to use a weedkiller or pesticide.

~Adapt the **Fukuoka** plan in your garden - or the tiniest courtyard plot... and you can forever forget about digging, weeding or labouring. Just toss new seeds or transplants in every three months (and I mean toss), and let nature do all your work! (This goes several steps *beyond* any conventional 'no dig' method you may have heard of.)

~Use the **ISP** (Intensive Successional Planting) method... and harvest delicious edible leaves, roots or flowers from every square inch of even the smallest garden - 365 days in the year.

And much, much more...

2. You acquire little-known gardening secrets

You gain exclusive access through the newsletter to my personal and private **research**, month by month, as I test these ideas in practice.

I've spent 31 years compiling a massive library of over 50,000 proven, little-known and sometimes literally 'off the wall' ways to grow much higher yields of healthier edible plants, organically. With the least effort. With little or no cost (either to you or to the planet). And often in the worst possible soil (or none).

Now it's on a computerised database, *unique in the world.* And my new-found joy in my retirement is to *test* these ideas, for myself (and for you) in my own ½ acre "garden laboratory", here at Ivinghoe Aston in the Chiltern hills. And to share them with you.

No, I'm *not* a trained horticulturalist. So I try quirky ideas that so-called 'experts' would never dream of trying. (Is that because they learned all they know from colleges run by people as unimaginative as themselves? *Whoops... sorry*).

Yet often my weird ideas and 'green' alternatives work magnificently, in direct contradiction of the experts - and their textbooks.

As a Guild member, you'll be among the few people in the world to be privileged to discover and use them too.

True, occasionally I make mistakes. In fact, I make *hundreds* of mistakes - far more than the average gardener! That's because every year I try so many new ideas. But my 'mistakes' have often yielded me the most valuable discoveries - genuinely new breakthroughs - and I pass these original tips onto you.

> (In fact, when I tried 'expert advice' it usually failed. Have you too ever wondered why some writers of 'coffee table' gardening books echo each other? And because they've never done it themselves, they repeat advice that was *wrong in the first place!*)

I do it the hard way, under the worst conditions - so you don't have to.

No, I *don't* have ideal soil - or weather. (As you've read!) Quite the reverse. My **soil** is hard clay on top of chalk and flint. Yet I've grown bumper carrots and parsnips there, said to be impossible in clay and flint, plus every other imaginable vegetable too.

> (Including some you *can't* readily imagine: they're straight out of The Arabian Nights. I'll tell you how to grow them - even in the UK!)

As for **weather**... my garden in Ivinghoe Aston is the focus of Force 8 gales. They rush straight off our Chiltern hills to topple my bean trellises and blast-freeze my seedlings even in July. I'll show you how to 'weather proof' your garden, cheaply and easily - even without YeoPods (And no, you *won't* easily find these ideas elsewhere!)

3. You enjoy free seeds - the fresh bounty from my own garden

If I've grown a big crop of seeds from rare or heritage plants I'll tell you what I have and you can request what you'd like, and get it. *Free.*

By law, I cannot sell you these seeds. But when you're a Guild member, I can *give* them to you, as one friend to another. Free.

For example, one year I grew out no fewer than *110* different varieties of rare heirloom **beans**. They were incredibly prolific and tasted scrumptious. Yet virtually nobody else in the UK had even heard of them!

I also stored away pint after pint of rare **tomato** seeds - no fewer than 62 different heritage cultivars. Plus umpteen jars of other exotic **vegetable** seeds, almost never grown in the UK

That's far more seed than I can ever use in my ½ acre paddock garden. I store it meticulously in my three 'seed 'fridges' so its germination is excellent.

At time of writing, I'm trialling 15 new rare varieties of dwarf french beans, 84 climbing beans, three rare broad beans, a dozen new tomato cultivars, and eight new lettuces. Most are 'heirlooms' - impossible to buy. And I'll report my results in the newsletter.

Those precious heirloom seeds can be yours, free, when you join the Guild

No, I'm *not* competing with the superb HDRA Seed Library (nor, so professional is it, would I *ever* dream of doing so). I'm proud to be an HDRA Seed Guardian myself and, if you're not already a member of the HDRA, *I urge you to become one at once!* But the more of those irreplaceable vegetable seeds we can place into safe hands - by whatever means - the better we can preserve them for our children.

Every season, I'll tell you what rare seed I have - and you can place your request. And I'll send you what I've got, free. In a typical year, my catalogue might have upwards of 120 *different* rare seed varieties. (No, truthfully, I can't make any guarantees on this. Gardening is full of wonderful surprises, but also failures. If I have it, you'll have it. If not, then not... *but there's always next season!*)

4. Join now as a Charter Member and accept FREE a

big Companion Planting wallchart plus a *Lazy Kitchen Garden* Planning calendar, valued together at £11.95.

I created these two unique guides for my own use, so they're unusually practical and inventive, as you'd expect. One side shows **companion planting** tips, the other is the **calendar**.

The wallchart is a big A2 size - approx 16.5in x 24 in (42cm x 60cm), laminated and waterproof, so you can hang it for permanent reference in your potting shed, greenhouse, conservatory or kitchen. What's more, the companion planting side is in full colour and (my wife says) very pretty it looks.

* **The Companion Planting chart** lists all your favourite kitchen garden vegetables (plus a few strange ones). It clearly shows which plants enhance the growth of others, when grown alongside, and which actively suppress each other.

I drew my research from many little-known sources but corrected it from my own experience.

(For example, would you really grow **horseradish** as a companion plant with potatoes, as some textbooks foolishly advise? You'll never grow another plant in that plot, because next year the horseradish takes over and you'll never dig it all out!

But if you want to *contain* horseradish, mint, comfrey and other creeping plants... just ring them with **fennel**. It suppresses everything. And so on... just follow the wallchart.)

It also incorporates a **crop rotation** and **sowing calendar** for each plant, so you'll never again be uncertain what should go where - or when.

Plus... it gives proven tips for **succession planting, catch cropping** and **intercropping** for all popular vegetables - so you can grow more food in a small area than you ever thought possible, year round.

   * <u>**The Lazy Kitchen Gardener calendar**</u> gives you ample space to jot in your own 'must do' tasks for every month, and also reminds you what should be sown or transplanted at every time in the year. It abounds with so many imaginative ideas, you just have to see it!

> For example, every month has five weeks, so you have an extra week to catch up with what you should have done that month. This gives you eight extra weeks over the year, so you can raise three successive crops of sweet corn even in the UK... can't you? (I am nothing if not generous.) *Plus much, much more...*

> *I truly think this 'double purpose' wallplanner - which I'm not selling separately - is worth the cost of your subscription in itself.*

In total, here is what you get in your bumper package

   * Six big entertaining **newsletters** every year, chockful of 'lazy gardening' tips

   * Continual access through the newsletter to **rarely-before published secrets** to make your gardening a snap - tested wherever possible in my own garden

   * Periodic gifts of **free heirloom or rare seeds**, never available for sale in the UK. (I'll include my latest FREE seed catalogue in your Welcome Pack!)

   * A large decorative **wallplanner** that all by itself shows you exactly what to grow, where, when and how

But I've kept the best till last...

   When you join the Village Guild as a Charter Member by bank standing order or credit card mandate, I'll welcome you with a **gift certificate of £20** to apply against your subscription - not just this year but *every year afterwards!*

So whereas the 'public' price is £79 per annum, your joining fee with the gift certificate is merely £59 per annum - and I'll honour that special low fee throughout the life of your subscription.

I can afford to do that *only* because you're a valued existing customer, and a reader of my book. So I don't have to pay the expense of renting mailing lists or hiring a mailing house.

But when I go out to the general public, my response is lower (because the public doesn't know me) and my costs are higher (because I'll be using a mailing house) so I have to charge £79.

And I can afford that big welcome gift *only* on subscriptions taken out by standing order or credit card mandate. Truly, I won't make much (or any) profit in the first year of your subscription - I'll only make a modest profit on your renewal.

A continuous payment mandate will help me renew your membership automatically and... *without waking up my wife.* (You see, I tend to clomp around the house at midnight when I'm doing paperwork - like oodles of renewal invoices. If you've ever run your own small business at home, you'll know how very important it is to preserve marital felicity...)

Your satisfaction is totally guaranteed

In fact, I give you *two* **personal guarantees** that you'll be - not just delighted, but *astounded!*

Guarantee One... when you send me your completed standing order or credit card mandate I'll rush you at once a big **Welcome Kit** containing the current newsletter plus your free wallplanner and heirloom seed catalogue. *But I won't process your money for 30 days!*

You'll have a full month to review those materials. If *for any reason whatever* you don't want to continue with your membership simply drop me a line, even a postcard, within 30 days with your name and address plus the words "Please cancel my membership".

I'll throw away your application, and I'll never take your money (you have my personal word on that)... *but you can still keep all those valuable materials I've sent you.*

Guarantee Two... if at any time in the year you feel you don't want to proceed with a further year's membership, just write to me accordingly and I'll take no further subscription.

Incidentally, I know you don't *really* need this information but... my accountants are Foxley Kingham, Prospero House, 46/48 Rothesay Road, Luton LU1 1QZ (that's also my registered office address); my bank is the HSBC, George Street, Luton LU1 2AP; the Village Guild Ltd is registered in England No: 3781310; and my inside leg measurement is... no, I'm *sure* you don't need that.

Apply now and enjoy your Welcome Kit at once

Simply complete the membership application that follows, send it to me using my Freepost address (no postage needed in the UK) and I'll pack up and post your Welcome Kit straightaway.

And I will welcome you *personally!*

John Yeoman

The Village Guild Ltd, FREEPOST ANG7357, Ivinghoe Aston, Leighton Buzzard, LU7 9ZZ. (No stamp needed in the UK.) 01525 221492. E-mail: john@villageguild.co.uk

Apply now for Charter Membership in the Village Guild

YES, John, I accept your invitation to join the Village Guild under the personal assurance of your two Guarantees.

I understand I will receive six idea-packed **newsletters** every year, *plus* access to thousands of rarely before published **gardening secrets**, *plus* my choice from as many as 120 free **heirloom** or **rare seeds** annually, *plus* a big free **wallplanner** as my joining gift. My membership fee *will not be processed for 30 days* following receipt of my application.

Surname   First name   Title

Address

Postcode

I prefer to join by:
1. Bankers Order

To: The Manager **X**   **X** Bank
Bank address **X**
                                                                X

Please pay to the order of the Village Guild Ltd a/c no 01666088 at HSBC Bank, 63 George St., Luton LU1 2AP, 40-30-32, the sum of £59 immediately and at annual intervals thereafter the sum of £59, being my subscription to the Village Guild and debit my/our account accordingly until countermanded by me in writing.

Bank a/c no: Bank sort code:

Bank account in name of:

Signature X   X Date

Note: you will find the information above on your cheque book. Bankers Orders are valid only for UK banks. Overseas members please use credit card method.

2. Credit Card

Please charge my Visa/MasterCard card. I authorise you to debit my credit card with the amount of £59 for my first year's membership and thereafter at annual intervals with the sum of £59, being a saving of £20 on the public fee, until further notice from me in writing.

My card no is: _____ Expiry: ___/___

Name as on card:

Address where my card statement is received, if different from above:

Signature X   X Date

Please return (postpaid) to: The Village Guild Ltd, FREEPOST ANG7357, Ivinghoe Aston, Leighton Buzzard, Beds LU7 9XX, UK